A Thousand Paths to Good Luck

A Thousand Paths to
good luck

David Baird

MQP

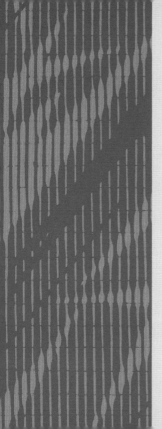

Contents

Introduction

Some people have all the luck—at least that is how it seems at times. And others seem to have little or no luck at all. Some of us are lucky in love; others get all the breaks, take the risks, and win all the wagers.

But what is this elusive thing we call luck? Can there really be such a thing or is it simply a case of being in the right place at the right time or maybe even a series of coincidences? Is it merely the result of various risks taken, of the decisions and choices we've made, of learning from our mistakes and being prepared for what lies ahead?

Suppose, for a moment, that there was no such word as "luck" but instead a world filled with opportunities for all of us—if only we were bright enough to recognize them when they arise, then make the right decisions, and take the correct action. Then luck comes within the grasp of us all, no matter how unlucky we may have felt before. Luck becomes less of a mystical, magical phenomenon and instead becomes the way in which others perceive the results of our actions and achievements. For, in truth, there is nothing without toil and no winning without taking part.

We are limiting our vision of luck if we think of it as being merely a big lottery win or coming first. Good luck is within our reach, if we only take time to read the signs along the path.

Good luck!

Are You
Feeling
Lucky?

Life has a tendency to confront us with ordeals, some of which will prove to be the worst imaginable. Yet we come through them without actually having been killed by them and for this, we can count ourselves extremely lucky.

Luck blossoms unexpectedly and must, for its brief duration, be enjoyed where it grows.

We are inclined to accept the results of our endeavors as being the result of our perception, intelligence, wisdom, discipline, and hard work, and pay little heed to chance, accident, passion, coincidence, and luck.

It is easier to walk away empty handed when you realize that in some form or other, one always ends up paying for one's good fortune.

Nothing is as insulting to someone who succeeds after much practice and developing their ability to focus under pressure as telling them how lucky they have been.

Those who are kind and generous to others are more likely to be offered assistance in return in times of need. Such a generous person is far more likely to be perceived by others as lucky.

It is said that one should never worship false idols and Luck is perhaps the worst for it is worshipped mainly by the idle.

We all need regular reminding that we are better than we think we are. We see successful people around us and view them as super or superior to us, yet they are no different to us apart from being lucky enough to have developed a belief in themselves and all that they do.

**Luck has no confines.
One person's wrecked life captured
in words may become tomorrow's
bestseller or Hollywood blockbuster.**

Travel life with your eyes and ears open.
You never know what you might be
lucky enough to overhear or witness.

The good of other times let people state;
I think it lucky I was born so late.

Ovid

A truly lucky person is rarer than a white crow.

Luckless is the country in which the symbols
of procreation are the objects of shame,
while the agents of destruction are honored!

Cyrano de Bergerac

Luck is not something to base all one's belief in, neither should we place all our trust in it, but to deny its existence would be just as extreme as doing either of these things.

Luck is an empty vessel and needs to be skillfully guided. Wait at the shore for it to find its way to you and you will wait forever in vain.

Lucky charms are merely emotional crutches. Remember as you stroke your rabbit's foot for luck that it was anything but lucky for the poor rabbit.

Luck, bad and good, will always be with us and either way comes to us at a cost. The intelligent who recognize this accept luck in whatever shape or form it comes. The less intelligent among us accept only the good luck and see bad luck as an abandonment.

You may choose to blame your failure to succeed today on getting out of the wrong side of the bed, or you may have the good luck to realize, before it's too late, that things aren't going well because of your own stubbornness.

There is many a politician and world leader who curses their luck for having been born honest.

Help luck: watch for opportunities and open yourself to possibilities.

When a person no longer has reason to trust in themselves they instead choose to trust in luck.

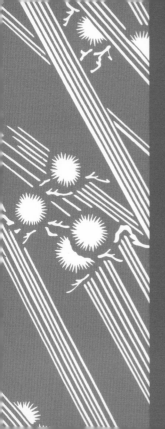

When we blame the consequences of our own risky behavior upon bad luck we are doing nothing more than avoiding responsibility for our actions.

At times such as these it is not luck that lets us down but ourselves.

Luck never gives; it only lends.

Life is made up of choices and where there are no obvious choices there is always a fifty-fifty chance that luck will come into play.

Luck is having people around you who love and care for you and the heart and good sense to recognize it.

Life is not a fairy tale. Not every scenario ends
"Happily ever after," neither is it a disaster
movie with a "They'll never make it" ending.
Seek out opportunities and chances and
with a little luck, things may just work out right.

**Luck is all about making the right
decisions when chance or opportunity
is in front of you.**

Good luck beats early rising.

Those who go through life believing everything is a consequence of their luck are destined to die of hope. If your actions lead to you ending your days on the gallows at noon, you can always blame your bad luck for being there and hope that with better luck, the noose will break or the clock will fail to strike!

Those of us who have been lucky enough to experience wonderful people and wonderful places will carry them with us wherever we go and for the rest of our lives.

With a productive imagination and an ability to put thoughts into action, there is little need for luck.

Luck, when analyzed too closely, ceases to be. Those who crane their necks in search of the right circumstances, the right name, the right number, the right time, or the right place will always be facing in the opposite direction to their chances.

To die is different from
what anyone supposed,
and luckier.

Walt Whitman

**Brag little, lose well,
own up, pay up,
and if you must win,
do so gently.**

Luck is the constant
companion of those
who consistently give
their very best.

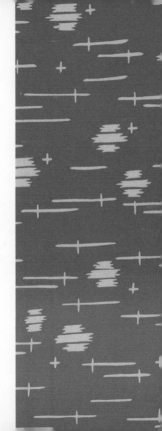

All spiders, except tarantulas, are omens of good luck. The larger the spider, the bigger the rewards.

If one wishes to witness luck in action it is better to risk all at cards or dice and stand to win or lose, for there is no luck in the workplace save the work itself. The results are self-made.

Relationships are said to be based upon trust and to a certain degree this is true, but the rest lies in having the good luck to find the right people.

Scratch off the surface of bad luck and you will find a chance to turn that luck around.

Can we estimate the amount
of good luck that may come our way?
The only thing that is certain is that
unless we have a willingness to act,
nil would be the safest answer.

You can't plea bargain with superstition.

The patron of misogynistic good luck is Adam for he had no mother-in-law to contend with.

Never underestimate the significance of diligence for it is the mother of good luck.

Nothing seems to bring greater pleasure
than the sight of an old adversary who is
down on his luck.

Luck is a slippery creature.
It seems to seek out those who flee
and flees from those who seek it.

Luck is having
good food on your table
and the taste buds to
appreciate it.

Many people consider certain numbers to be lucky or unlucky. They go out of their way and often to great expense to obtain what they consider to be "lucky" phone numbers, license plates, or even addresses. Of course, the number can do little more than make that person feel lucky but they should not be surprised if, when placing $7 on horse number 7 in the 7th race, it comes in 7th. We tend to classify a person winning a lottery as lucky even though there was inevitably going to be a winner sometime, somewhere, so there was in fact nothing lucky about someone winning.

Do not take anyone's word for it but discover for yourself that the harder you work, the luckier you will seem to become.

Ask yourself whether the purpose of your life is to wait to be lucky or whether it is more important to have mattered, to have made some difference to the world by having been here, to have been productive and inspiring to others. The luckiest person to have lived is the person who can see self-fulfillment in their own lifetime.

One person's superstition is likely to be another's bad luck. For example, some believe that a bed changed on Friday will bring bad dreams. Depending on how you look at things, if you stay in a hotel on a Friday you won't get any sleep or, alternatively, you will sleep well in less than fresh sheets!

A person's need does not necessarily make them a better or more justified contender for good luck. But to the observer, when luck comes to those in need it is somehow seen as being better than when luck comes to those who are already considered fortunate.

Luck's infatuation is with efficiency.

Luck will come to every one of us at least once in our lifetime but many of us can't be bothered to open the door when it comes knocking.

Do everything the best you can and you may be lucky enough to discover that you are able to do it better than you thought you could.

An ounce of luck is more valuable than a pound of gold.

Mankind is capable of doing almost anything imaginable. His shortfall is that he rarely knows what it is he wishes to do.

In reality nobody is going to come to you to make you rich or to make you famous. These come as the direct results of hard graft, many put-downs, and countless setbacks, which, if the talent survives along with the will to go on, might just run you into a coincidental spot of good luck.

**Luck takes hard work—
the harder one works,
the luckier one gets.**

In a world so skeptical about luck
and superstition how is it that eight
out of every ten high-rise buildings
have no 13th floor? Why is there no
gate 13 at the airport and no 13th
aisle on the plane? Try and ask for
room 13 at an hotel and consider
the plight of Apollo 13.

The lazy person always seems prepared to estimate the industrious person's successes as good luck.

The very best luck any person can hope for is to have been born with the determination and ability to overcome any bad luck that life may throw at you.

Looking at luck objectively will illustrate that what we think of as luck will, in the main, tend to be against those who depend on it.

Luck is a very good word
if you put a P before it.

**Luck is actually rather predictable.
If one wants more luck one should
become more active and try to take
more chances. Often it is simply a
case of turning up or having a go.**

Luck has no history and no future.
Those who talk about it do not create it.
Those who have it now
may never have had it before
and may not have it tomorrow.

There is no such thing as luck.
It's a fancy name for being always at
our duty, and so sure to be ready when
good time comes.

Edward G. Bulwer-Lytton

Luck is meaningless until
that moment when one
amazes oneself with one's
own good luck.

Ask any failure and they will tell you success is just a matter of luck.

Luck itself leads nowhere.
It's what you do with it that
defines the destination.

Some people are born truly lucky. Content with hard work and its results they live twice as long as those who go through life worrying about their rotten luck. In effect they live two lifetimes, which is very good luck indeed.

When you have given your all, the full 100%, then luck is what you have left.

Whoever has the luck to be born
a character can laugh even at death.
Because a character will never die!
A man will die, a writer, the instrument
of creation: but what he has created
will never die!

Luigi Pirandello

Can we control luck? It is often said that luck
is about being in the right place at the right
time. Given that we can choose our timing
and locations perhaps luck can, to some
extent at least, fall within our control.

Everything in life seems to demand explanation, apart from good luck, which we are inclined to accept without question.

When we set about making things happen we externalize our inner self. This is perceived by the idle as luck.

When you seem to be making slow progress, the impatient person will curse his luck at not being able to go full steam ahead. The objective person will enjoy the pace, wary of the possibility that they may be headed in the wrong direction.

Luck demands that we adapt ourselves to pass through hard times as bravely and cheerfully as possible.

When we step back
and analyze our lives
and our luck we
discover that those
good things,
the friendships,
the relationships, and
the opportunities,
did not come about
purely by chance but
by careful and
deliberate steps.

Who can tell what is good or bad luck?

Zen

If you insist upon developing a love of luck then you must also develop a love of detail to foresight!

The goddess of luck favors people of action.

Luck requires our help in that we open our minds and hearts and remain ever watchful for opportunities.

Always spit on anything new before using it to make it lucky.

A lucky mind is patient yet restless.
Ease and vanity repel luck.

**We must believe in luck.
For how else can we explain the
success of those we don't like?**

Jean Cocteau

It takes a clever person indeed
to turn the accidental to some good
and a fool to turn great luck
to disadvantage.

We are all equally susceptible to good and bad luck. Those of us who persist through the bad luck tend to be the ones who are there ready when good luck comes along.

Luck must be accepted for what it is: a belief in cause and effect, not a shallow belief in circumstances.

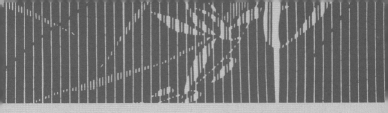

The worst luck of all is to have been born superstitious.

If you are unlucky enough to be superstitious then your bad luck will always be redoubled on a Friday and tripled if that Friday happens to be the 13th!

Now here's a quandary! It is said that if you throw back the first fish you catch, then you'll be lucky the whole day fishing. But it's also said that if you count the number of fish you caught, you will catch no more that day. So how do you know it's your first fish if you aren't counting? Seems that the superstitious are destined to starve!

Some people believe that if you find a magic lamp and rub it, a genie will appear and grant three wishes. If they were truly lucky, they'd see the telltale stains on the carpet where those who tried before them achieved nothing more than spilling lamp oil.

Luck is momentary, transient, and without reason. It only takes a stock market crash to unfold the bizarre spectacle of countless suicides dressed in fur and dripping with gold carted off in disbelief by the happier poor.

**Luck is made—
one can stand by the river
and wait for the fish to jump
into one's arms, or bait a line
and cast it where you know
the fish are feeding.**

Work hard every day and you will get lucky.

Some folk want their luck buttered.
Thomas Hardy

Luck means nothing if it comes in the form of an opportunity you are unable to handle when it is given to you.

The same plot of land will provide either a snack or a banquet. It is not about luck but more to do with honest toil and patience.

Is it not curious that we attribute our good luck to our own good sense and our bad luck to the gods.

The world is getting to be such a dangerous place, a man is lucky to get out of it alive.

W. C. Fields

Luck can never be truly known. The only thing we can know for certain about it is that it will change. Accept this and you will never be let down by it.

Getting away with one's good luck unnoticed is about as easy as plucking a chicken without it realizing.

Luck is like truth— a fruit which is better harvested when ripe.

The curious thing about some people is the way they seem to be in such a rush to meet bad luck halfway.

Is it luck that while some have persevered others have given up in despair?

Is it luck that people who have attained things worth having in this world have worked while others have idled?

Luck is purpose guided by tenacity.

Every system that works well, on the whole, is more than a lucky accident. It is derived from a long process of trial and error and never-ceasing responses to change.

When one develops and puts
into practice the attributes of
self-denial, industriousness,
and a focused sense of purpose,
the results are more likely to be
success than failure, and of course
such success will be attributed by
others to good luck.

Luck is about taking advantage of any particular situation at exactly the right moment. To do this one must develop an attitude of "Oh look it's here!" and rid oneself of the "Too late it's gone…" syndrome!

Nothing drives home one's own inadequacies as much as those well-meant words, "Oh dear, bad luck!"

All things founded on luck alone are devoid of greatness.

Luck is a dividend of sweat and toil.

The best luck to have is that of having talent. The best talent to have is the talent to see talent in others and to be able to harness it.

The secret to a peaceful life is to conduct it in such a manner that luck cannot possibly interfere with it either way.

Luck—whichever way it falls, it's always held to blame.

Any person of good energy and spirit who remains upright, conscientious, and diligent will be perceived as lucky whether they win or lose.

It seems to help us, whether we're on the rise or on the fall, to believe that no matter how good we are are, there's always a great deal of luck involved.

One can waste an entire lifetime depending on luck but, without doubt, the very best luck of all is the luck that we make for ourselves.

A tragic life ends,
for the bad among us,
unhappily, and for the good
it is sure to end unluckily.

It's considered good luck to find a four-leaf clover. Clover is believed to protect humans and animals from the spells of magicians and the ill-doings of fairies.

Better to be respected in life for one's merit than one's luck.

Sometimes people are unlucky enough to have been born too lucky. For example, they are born too pretty or too successful—and are considered by others as being just too lucky and therefore suffer their indifference, jealousy, anger, and displeasure.

The greatest luck is in happiness but it is also fragile. Never push your luck by trying to define it.

Bad luck sometimes appears to be magnetic in its nature, especially when we can witness others running headlong into regular misfortunes that always seem to be designed to happen to somebody else.

Where there is a person who is constantly discovered lamenting their own ill luck, chances are you will be witnessing someone who is not unlucky at all but rather someone who is suffering the consequences of their own negligence.

Luck,
Fate, and
Destiny

One's destiny is not a question or matter of chance. It is the result of one's choices. One does not wait around for one's destiny to happen—one must get out there and achieve it.

Our actions can best be described as the seeds of fate, which, when planted and nurtured, grow into our destiny.

Fate will fall on you unless you act.

From time to time there appear on the face of the earth men of rare and consummate excellence, who dazzle us by their virtue, and whose outstanding qualities shed a stupendous light. Like those extraordinary stars of whose origins we are ignorant, and of whose fate, once they have vanished, we know even less, such men have neither forebears nor descendants: they are the whole of their race.

Jean de La Bruyère

Don't blame fate for dealing you the wrong cards. Play them as well as they can possibly be played and bluff for all you're worth.

To the observer, everything evil would seem to be the workings of fate, while there seems to be an art involved with everything that is good.

Whenever we find ourselves limited in any way, fate is the word that springs to our lips.

We strive to retain our youth and innocence and to obtain wealth and good standing. Yet youth, wealth, high birth, and inexperience are all sources of potential ruin. Consider then the fate of those in possession of all four at any stage of their life.

Fate, not choice, is what tends to make us adventurers.

Everything is changing daily and none of us can expect to be exempt from this common fate. It results in us having constant changes in our fortune and experiencing gradual decay.

We are not, as we seem to want to believe, prisoners of fate. To think so makes us prisoners of our own minds.

Fate for some soars like an eagle and for others less fortunate it slithers like a snake in the grass.

Do not live to seek enjoyment or travel through life in sorrow. Instead take action to ensure that each new tomorrow sees you further along the path than you were today.

He who asks fortune-tellers the future
unwittingly forfeits an inner intimation of
coming events that is a thousand times
more exact than anything they may say.
He is impelled by inertia, rather than curiosity,
and nothing is more unlike the submissive
apathy with which he hears his fate revealed
than the alert dexterity with which the man of
courage lays hands on the future.

Walter Benjamin

**If you can't change your fate then
it's time to change your attitude.**

There is always potential.

Fate rules the affairs of men. Unfortunately it does so in no recognizable order.

For a person to be the master of their fate they must first wish to be so.

All the fears and hopes of humanity hang on fate.

If we were to change the name Planet Earth to Spaceship Earth then perhaps everybody would see that we are all part of one common fate and that each and every one of us had better pull their weight.

All human things are subject to decay,
and when fate summons,
monarchs must obey.

John Dryden

Fate is "unpenetrated" cause. It is the facts that we shall eventually discover but which have not yet passed under the scrutiny of thought.

Those who have worked hard to succeed and put it all down to luck are kidding themselves.

What is the fate of the lucky man? Throw him into the sea and he is likely to come up with a pearl clenched between his teeth.

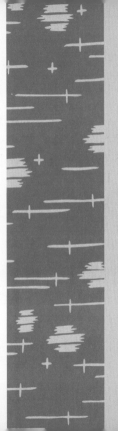

Superstition, bigotry, and prejudice, ghosts though they are, cling tenaciously to life; they are shadows armed with tooth and claw. They must be grappled with unceasingly, for it is a fateful part of human destiny that it is condemned to wage perpetual war against ghosts. A shadow is not easily taken by the throat and destroyed.

Victor Hugo

Develop a heart that is open to whatever fate may deal you and then get up and commence doing. Seek to achieve and instead of waiting, pursue.

Ordinary people tend to be passive and consider themselves to be masters of their own fate, yet they feel helpless against greater events and stand like terrified animals in the path of an oncoming tornado when they should be endeavoring to influence events or get out of the way.

If we leave everything to chance, luck, fate, and destiny, it is like getting into your car, closing your eyes, and folding your arms then pressing the accelerator and hoping to be lucky enough to reach your exact destination without mishap.

Do not sit there and take what life throws at you. Sometimes our fate needs a good, firm shake-up.

On the death of a friend, we should consider that the fates through confidence have devolved on us the task of a double living, that we have henceforth to fulfill the promise of our friend's life also, in our own, to the world.

Henry David Thoreau

Our fate depends less these days upon our birth or marital family than the workplace in which we spend the most alert hours of our best years.

If a person believes they are destined to drown, then chances are they will probably do so even in a puddle or a bowl of soup.

Sometimes our arms are so busy warding off the despair of what fate has dealt us that we are unable to embrace the potential that lies in our future—let it go.

The fate of love is that it will always be perceived as too little too late or too much too soon.

**If one thing could define our fate
it would be our character.**

**When we become masters of our
own fate we cannot complain of a
hard sentence.**

As humans we are blessed with the power
to control our thoughts and attitudes. This
makes us the masters of our fate and the
captains of our souls.

He either fears his fate too much,
Or his deserts are small,
That dares not put it to the touch,
To gain or lose it all.

James Graham

The strong advance boldly to meet
dangerous circumstances head on
while the weaker grow agitated.
The superior person stands up
to fate and endures such
circumstances resolutely,
comforted by inner certainty.

The worst form of slavery is the strict belief in fate. One spends one's life on bent knees, hoping to move gods with prayers, when one could move mountains if only one were prepared to take a chance and stand up.

Into each life some rain must fall.

Henry Wadsworth Longfellow

Trouble is not a bringer of bad luck.
It brings its share of joys and sorrows,
each enjoyable in their own way.

**Perhaps all beings are fated
to happiness.**

**A lack of, or abundance of,
morality is not fate, just a
weakness of the brain.**

The fate of any country lies in the hands of
those responsible for educating its people.

The fate
and genius
of a nation
is changed
through
commerce
and politics,
not luck.

Be more like the cat whose tail wags contempt at fate.

All who have meditated on the art of governing mankind have been convinced that the fate of empires depends on the education of youth.

Aristotle

Our fate can be overcome by having patience under it.

It is mankind's luck, good or bad, that some backroom utterings made in the right circumstances stand the chance of determining the fate of a nation.

Tempted fate will leave the loftiest star.

Lord Byron

Fate rises often from the least momentous things, just as rivers may rise out of springs.

It is mankind's predestined folly to make his own fortunes and call them fate.

Only the fool seeks to discover their fate. Where there is already joy, that is where fate has been best concealed.

Fate is nothing but the deeds committed in a prior state of existence.

Ralph Waldo Emerson

Believe this: any person would find their sorrows much increased if their future fortunes were known to them today.

If you must believe
in fate, it would be
better to believe in
it for your good.

**None of us can
possibly know what
fate has in store for
us but we can
believe in our
hearts that it shall
be great and live
with that in mind.**

Fate just keeps on happening.

When an inner situation is not made consciou, it appears outside as fate.
Carl Jung

Can we change our fate?
Only when the will of
human reason is stronger
than fate can we hope to
change it.

Fate will lead those
who will follow it
and drag those
who would resist.

Full of wisdom are the ordinations of fate.

Friedrich von Schiller

**Fate deals us the hand
and we play the cards.**

Accept fate then move on.

Avoid the temptation to yield
to self-pity. Acting like a victim
threatens our future.

Wherever the fates lead us let us follow.

Virgil

Fate is a chain reaction. It is the cause to every effect, the reason things are as they are, and why the world must and does carry on.

The unluckiest fate of mankind is that during the best of times or the greatest spells of evil we remain constant in our fearing for the worst.

With luck, when the time arises, we find the strength within us to defy fear, to challenge our fate, to refuse to compromise even with death, and to be heroic.

There is no antidote to fate and no armor to protect us against it.

The very same flexibility and ease which make people's friendships so agreeable while they endure, make them all the easier to destroy and forget at the drop of a hat.

Happiness and good luck balance precariously and it takes only a stroke of fate, a few badly chosen words, some scrawl on a piece of paper, the death of someone, or a person's change of mind to leave us alone and destitute in the twinkling of an eye.

One should replace one's dependence upon fate with a clear set of objectives. These will not determine our future but if we remain committed to them they can provide us with direction, and allow us to utilize our energy and resources to make a future.

We are lucky when we realize in time that before us are a finite number of years left to live out. Such fate is always at our side. We must endeavor to make good use of our time while it still remains within our power to do so.

To find one's path through the minefield of fate and arrive at lucky outcomes, one must learn to recognize one's ideas and get beyond the state of contemplating them by taking some form of external or inner action.

Our ideas are the most powerful thing about us and the surest path to luck, for they demand change and action. They concentrate our vision and determine our priorities and must not be left to chance.

There can be no luck where life is in such chaos that we can no longer determine our moral and intellectual priorities.

It is the fate of the great ones of this earth to only be truly appreciated after they are gone.

All of us go to our final resting places without this or that or having not achieved this or that thing. Let this thought grant you a happier fate.

Man is man because he is free to operate within the framework of his destiny. He is free to deliberate, to make decisions, and to choose between alternatives.

Theodore Roosevelt

So long as a person continues to think, the intellect will keep him free from the perils of fate.

Pass not today in vain for it will not pass this way again.

If everything is left to fate then those who have the least will forever continue to add to the treasury of the wealthy.

It seems the fate of all great souls to live alone.

We are luckiest when we are able to accept the things to which fate binds us, and to love the people with whom fate brings us together, and do so with all our heart.

Love is not something that lies within our buffet of choices but is the centerpiece to fate's feast.

The aim, if reached or
not, makes great the life:
try to be Shakespeare,
leave the rest to fate!

Robert Browning

**When we become
disenchanted with
fate, we turn instead
to characterizing
our lives through
the processes of
rationalization and
intellectualization.**

Work out your own
salvation. Do not
depend on others.

Buddha

It is not accidental that mankind's
most popular art is more intimate
than monumental.

One solves few earthbound problems by transferring all the sublime values of public life entirely into the transcendental realm of one's mystical or spiritual life. Such meditative transcendence is to be encouraged for the individual, but it takes real physical brotherly love and positive personal human interaction to straighten out the world.

A world without fate is like a thought without a world.

To be lucky in love one must bellow at fate, be reckless, and run on impulse without a care about the immortal soul and never stopping to dwell about the ultimate.

The unpredictability that engulfs human affairs is the by-product of our processes and has little to do with fate.

Mankind seems to be content to accept that his fate was to have been wrong and to stand in that wrongness doing nothing about trying to move away from it.

All of us are at some time the masters of our fate.

Fate is a trickster often against us in our hour of need. It grants us too late that which we begged for.

It is the saddest fate of all that we allow our fate to be shaped by politicians when history has illustrated that people of greatness do not go in for politics. Then the stark realization sets in that our fate is being left to those without ideals and without greatness.

The best way to learn the true value of those gifts that are useful to life is to have been born fated to experience poverty at first hand.

We are the product of our thoughts and actions. Public opinion means little or nothing to us but what we think of ourselves will shape our fate.

If you wish to experience a moment of being in control of your fate, go out into the world of people and say something nice to someone or do something kind for somebody then stand back and watch the chain reaction.

You cannot rebake a burnt cake but you can make another one with greater confidence and better luck.

There is no luck in a doctrine which expounds that the only way to Paradise or Heaven is through personal sacrifice or the sacrificing of others. Those who follow this risk everything while those who would preach this are the last ones prepared to take the gamble themselves.

Worship fate and you will become a slave to fate; then all that will be left is time, death, and ruinous thoughts.

Each of us carries within us everything we need—our fate, our future, our entire world. We are never alone having these and no matter how far we may fall we can always help ourselves and still have the capacity to help someone else who's down there.

In truth, whatever comes to us, whether good or bad, is often less to do with fate and more the result of our own doing or our lack of action.

To subdue fate one must exert all possible human strength and if, after all this effort, success is still not achieved, then at least no one else can be blamed.

It is less
important
what our
fate is
than how
we become
masters of it.

To become truly free we must develop our will to rise above everything else: climate and the elements, our environment, tyranny, culture, influence, temperament, mood, family, friends, power, everything. This is where we will discover our true fate, our character.

A person's fate is their own temper.
Benjamin Disraeli

One's greatest dread should be of accepting meaninglessness as one's fate.

The fate of truth is to begin as heresy and end as superstition.

Let your philosophy be fortitude! To bear is to conquer our fate.

I know my fate. One day there will be associated with my name the recollection of something frightful—of a crisis like no other before on earth, of the profoundest collision of conscience, of a decision evoked against everything that until then had been believed in, demanded, sanctified. I am not a man I am dynamite.

Friedrich Nietzsche

The most curious, inspiring, and terrifying notion regarding man is that his most irrevocable decisions will inevitably spring from a state of mind which is destined not to last.

The very fact that we live means we are destined for something.

It is the fate of mankind to come and go in the tides of time, but we leave our destined lineaments permanent forever and ever.

Imagine if every act which appears to us an act of our own will, is related to the entire course of history and was predestined from the beginnings of eternity.

If you believe it
is your destiny
to live out
your life as a
prisoner of
your mind then
furnish it well.

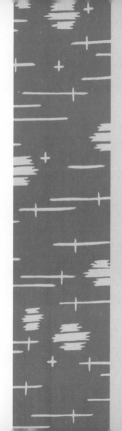

Luckily there are those who are destined to reason well and then there are those who are destined to reason wrongly; and those who are destined not to reason at all. Then, unfortunately, there are others who are destined to persecute all those who reason.

If you are really Master of your Fate,
it shouldn't make any difference to you
whether Cleopatra or the Bearded Lady
is your mate.

Ogden Nash

All are created equal in that each of us is predestined to have our own free will.

We cannot take to our graves that which we have accumulated during our lives. The person who dies rich, dies in a meaningless state compared to those who go to their rest having sowed their riches to benefit the poor.

Some are lucky to have been born able to bear what the world dishes out to them. To do so is to possess the ability to conquer one's fate.

Upon the conduct of each depends the fate of all.

Luck Is a Risky Business

If you are courageous and take a few risks, you will be lucky enough to accomplish something in life.

When a woman marries again it is because
    she detested her first husband.
When a man marries again it is because he
    adored his first wife.
Women try their luck; men risk theirs.

Oscar Wilde

When we take chances, we stand to lose. But we will never win anything if we never enter the game.

Ignore those who would talk you down. Take big chances, make big choices. Michelangelo painted the ceiling of the Sistine Chapel—it would have been easier to decorate the floor.

Inside all of us dwell the little voices of fear; they don't hesitate to tell us that others are better looking than us, cleverer, and better connected. Do not listen to them.

The luckiest people follow paths that not only interest them but that also accommodate love, sensitivity, and cooperation with others.

It is not by luck but by the strength of our convictions that we are able to move others by our efforts.

The further away from danger we are, the braver we seem to become. Just because we are not unlucky does not mean we are lucky or vice versa.

If we make our life based upon success or failure, we risk never being worthy of our own respect, let alone that of others.

Follow your intuition. It is the unexplored wilderness that lies within you and this is where we discover our true and potential self.

One should never worry about failing now and then. It's the surest sign there is that you've been playing it too safe up to that point.

A person's life can improve dramatically when they take a few chances. The first and most difficult risk one can take is to be honest with oneself.

Most people live and die with the music of their life never played, for they never dared to try.

To find our luck through risk, we must not only bite off more than we can chew but discover how to swallow and digest it at the same time.

Everything that is daring in our lives starts from within us.

Audacity can certainly inspire us to take on anything but it cannot make us do everything.

It is, in the main, less risky to put on your parachute before jumping out of the plane. If after all the preparation, checking it, and packing it properly, it doesn't open then at this point you might be tempted to consider whether your luck has run out on you.

We are all travelers and dream seekers.
We can follow the trails set by others or go
out into the wilderness and create our own.

Continuing when you are uncertain
of what you are doing is the kind of
risk that can lead to extraordinary
good luck.

We don't grow unless we take risks.
Every successful person's life, every
successful company, is riddled with
many failures.

All life is about chance, so take some.
Those who are most willing to do and dare
are the ones who generally get lucky and
go further in life.

Nobody ever got far on a sure thing.

No crime is so great as daring to excel.

Winston Churchill

Playing safe is often the least safe option. When the tide turns it is unwise to stand still while everyone else makes for higher ground.

The surest way to learn the game is to play it for more than you can comfortably afford to lose.

Every time the world moves forward it is because somebody is willing to put their neck on the line and risk trying something new.

Even the tortoise must stick his neck out if he hopes to make any progress.

In business, it is fundamental to understand that the buyer takes as many risks as the seller.

Good management goes further than good fortune. If you are lucky enough to understand thrift and management, a little will always go a long way. Without these there will never be enough.

At birth we are dealt a hand of cards
called Life. It must be played using the cards
we hold. Folding is not an option to us and in
order to stay in the game we must, from time
to time, take a few risks.

What good is it to
triumph without glory?
Or win without risk?

In order to conquer one must
dare, dare, and dare some more
or risk losing.

In any form of competition, from battle to ballroom dancing, one must participate until the final moment as though it might still be lost or won.

Persevere with audacity. It is a recipe for winning.

How will you ever know how far you can go if you are not prepared to risk going too far?

I dip my pen in the blackest ink, because I am not afraid of falling into my inkpot.

Ralph Waldo Emerson

Boldness alone is never enough.
Luck demands that cleverness accompany it.

If you want to stand out, it's not enough just to be different—you must be outstanding.

In the arena of human life the honors and rewards fall to those who show their good qualities in action.

Aristotle

You will discover that the main factor that leads people to assert that a thing cannot be done is their own unwillingness to give it a go.

A person who never budges should not expect a push.

Those who take risks, unaware of their actions, and who exercise little or no caution, are less guilty than vulnerable.

Every river would have been assumed too deep or fast flowing to cross had someone not risked finding out.

Where two paths meet and diverge, take the one less traveled and let your journey make a difference.

Do not yield to misfortunes, but advance as boldly to meet them, as your fortune permits you.

Virgil

As people become more successful, it becomes increasingly difficult for them to risk jeopardizing their security by taking new risks.

People would rather stop learning than risk failure.

On any scale, from the minute to the monumental, the thing that makes it satisfyingly triumphant is the element of uncertainty with which it was undertaken.

Risk a few shots and you may score a few hits. Take none, and you'll miss 100% of the time.

Prizes, rewards, riches, and power do not make any difference. It is what you choose to risk doing with them that leads to great things.

The more secure we attempt to make our world, the less so it seems to become.

When considering luck and risk, ponder the odds on this: is it more risky eating your way across any country than driving it?

Life is like sport. You have to get stuck in there, right in the thick of it, and take chances. The more you take, the greater the chance of winning through skill, or sheer luck— a win is a win.

Consider the artist, the composer, the painter, and the poet, all of whom dare to attempt anything their fancy suggests to them.

Passion takes great risks. A life without any mistakes is also a life without any dynamics.

It is easy to stop growing. Just tell yourself that you no longer want to take any risks.

Throughout history there have been countless examples where even the most absurd and reckless aspirations have led to extraordinary success.

It seems that for the majority of us, we are most alive when we are risking our all and feel luckiest afterward.

We are all granted the same choice in life to be safe and good or to take chances and dare to be great.

When we don't risk anything, we risk even more.

The greatest risk of all is not losing but the risk of doing nothing.

To the artist and businessperson the fight must be constant and one must be prepared to risk one's professional life every few months just to stay alive.

Try to think of failure as simply being a result that differs from the one you expected.

One person's life can be a daring adventure while another's can amount to nothing. Luck has little to do with it. One must risk doing something for luck to even enter the scenario.

Let my tombstone read that even when I failed I did so with panache and that where I go now it will not be among those timid souls who were never lucky enough to know victory and defeat.

Security does not exist in nature. Perhaps it is just a superstition that we need it and by avoiding all danger, perhaps we place ourselves at even greater risk than through our outright exposure to it.

There are risks and costs to a program of action, but they are far less than the long-range risks and costs of comfortable inaction.

John F. Kennedy

Be boldly decisive at the risk of being wrong. Nothing is worse than being right always too late.

Entrepreneurs are risk takers,
willing to roll the dice with
their money or reputation on
the line in support of an idea or
enterprise. They willingly assume
responsibility for the success
or failure of a venture and are
answerable for all its facets.
The buck not only stops at
their desks, it starts there too.

Victor Kiam

What is faith if not risk?
The greater our willingness, the
greater our potential to grasp.

When a person is first starting out in life, that is the time it is most dangerous not to take risks.

To win, you have to risk loss.
And to lose, you have to risk winning.

If one is inevitably going to make an error then it may as well be a good and memorable one—an error filled with promise and boldness.

God gave us necks in order that we occasionally stick them out.

What kind of person would dare to live where there is no risk?

There is no place in business, in sport, or art for anyone who is not a risk taker.

Make your choices and take your chances either way but do not hide your face from risk. For risk is a part of life and there would be no luck without it.

Never take foolish chances while remembering that nothing worth doing can be accomplished without taking any chance at all. Grasp this and your luck will turn.

Youth is a time for being unorthodox, for taking the greatest risks and being daring. When these attributes and approaches have dissipated it is a sure sign of having arrived at the steadiness and predictability that is middle age.

Step out of the darkness and run for daylight. Luck doesn't lurk in the shadows. It dances in the sunshine.

Have the courage to bet on your ideas.

Where there is a calculated risk, act.

Risk all and face the truth.

Risk all and act for yourself.

Sometimes you just have to try and do the thing on earth that it is hardest for you to do, whether it's persevering with an idea or risking making contact with an estranged relative or friend. Nothing ventured, nothing gained.

The deeper the water, the bigger the ship you can sail in it.

Without risk, how can we ever hope to expect more from ourselves than others believed was possible of us?

As life creates more and more opportunities for unlimited progress and growth, both corporate and personal, so too do the chances of failure increase, for these are not gifts but the results of risk.

Every noble acquisition is attended with its risks; he who fears to encounter the one must not expect to obtain the other.

Pietro Metastasio

To achieve anything great one must be prepared to balance precariously on the edge of the volcano and to dance on the brink of disaster.

The most difficult and fundamentally important risk we must take is to ensure that we are always honest with ourselves or luck will pass us by.

Who dares wins.

Dare to be wise.

The policy of being too cautious is the greatest risk of all.

Jawaharlal Nehru

The most important thing on the first step to heroics is to never allow yourself to discover the odds.

Great ends are destined to come to those who risk great hazards.

Little or no inspiration comes to those who remain cocooned within that which is comfortable and safe. There can be no development or growth without that essential ingredient: risk.

Luck comes to those who, once they have discovered what it is they do best, try something entirely new.

Whenever you feel you have something that is good and valid, it is time to put your ass on the line and stick your neck out. You may look strange but this is the courting dance for luck.

The key to getting lucky is to always try and take an educated risk.

Those who dare courageously to defend what they love are the happiest breed.

Daring is not safe against daring men.

Ovid

Do not mistake being rash with taking a calculated risk. One way leads to saving your bacon, the other way gets you fried.

You have to give up wanting to be a caterpillar if you want to take to the air.

If you want to gather roses expect to be pricked by a few thorns.

Where there is much to risk, there is also much to consider.

To do an evil act is base.
To do a good one without
incurring danger is common
enough. But it is part of a
good man to do great and
noble deeds though he risks
everything in doing them.

Plutarch

**There is no luck to be
found by erring on the
side of caution. Stay in
the valley and you will
never see the view from
the top of the hill.**

You will never learn to swim if you insist on keeping one foot on terra firma.

You have to be very lucky indeed if, when playing baseball, you imagine you can steal second base without taking your foot off first.

Dare and the world yields, and if it beats you the first time, dare it again and go on doing so until you succeed.

The best knowledge is bought for labor, and honor is sold for risk.

Those who live out their lives day to day in the safety of their established patterns are destined never to feel fulfilled. Their life is not about becoming lucky and successful but believing they are lucky if they manage to avoid failure.

If one knows exactly how wide a stream is, chances are one won't try to jump it. Without knowing how wide it is, most will attempt to jump it anyway and the majority who try will make it to the other side.

Show me those whose overwhelming
considerations are for safety and
security and I will show you those
who are not living life, but who are
the living dead.

Shallow men believe in luck.
Strong men believe in cause and effect.

Ralph Waldo Emerson

A lottery is a salutary instrument and a tax…laid on the willing only, that is to say, on those who can risk the price of a ticket without sensible injury, for the possibility of a higher prize.

Thomas Jefferson

He who spends himself in a worthy cause knows, in the end, the triumph of achievement.

Far better is it to dare mighty things, to win glorious triumphs, even though chequered by failure, than to rank with those poor spirits who neither enjoy much nor suffer much, because they live in a gray twilight that knows not victory nor defeat.

Theodore Roosevelt

Those who risk all to stand out from the rest of the crowd also risk becoming targets.

If you're happy with the ordinary then never risk the unusual.

Before taking your first step into any new venture consider custom and then take the opposite course. This way you will almost always do well.

Impossible kicks lead to magnificent goals and sometimes magnificent misses.

A person who sits idle and dares less risks doing nothing and achieving nothing.

The greatest risk any person can take is to dare to be themselves under any set of circumstances.

One can always stand a chance of winning against like-minded people but those who are prepared to take risks are the ones we are most likely to lose to.

To save all we must risk all.

Friedrich von Schiller

The person who gets all the fruit is the one who risks going out on a limb.

The path is smooth that leadeth on to danger.

William Shakespeare

The greatest wealth a person is given
is life itself. Playing it safe is the greatest
risk for we stand to waste everything.

**Taking risk is never the easier route
but it is certainly the sweeter option.**

When you are ready to risk a fall
you have reached the time in your
life to bravely dare.

**Be bold, be bold,
and everywhere be bold.**

Herbert Spencer

If we accept the theory that man evolved from the ape then he must have evolved from one that was prepared to take risks because the trees are still populated with monkeys.

It was a bold person that first ate an oyster.

Jonathan Swift

Audacity augments courage; hesitation, fear.

Publilius Syrus

Fortune

With wisdom we have it within our grasp to turn chance into good fortune.

Fortune's smile is expensive and is not formed through luck or chance. It must be earned and is the prize awarded for toil.

All honor to him who shall win the prize.
The world has cried for a thousand years.
But to him who tries and fails and dies,
I give great honor and glory and tears.

Joaquin Miller

Responsibility is something we all share —responsibility for our thoughts and our deeds. It is far too easy to remove the burden from our own shoulders and try to pin the blame on God, fate, fortune, or luck.

Luck and fortunes do not just happen.

Our misunderstanding of fortune is clear. Even when we make our own fortunes we still insist on calling them fate.

To accuse others for one's own misfortunes is a sign of want of education.
To accuse oneself shows that one's education has begun.
To accuse neither oneself nor others shows that one's education is complete.

Epictetus

The folly of mankind is clearly illustrated by the fact that the less we deserve good fortune, the more intensely we seem to hope for it.

Fortune is like glass—the brighter the glitter, the more easily broken.

Publilius Syrus

Only a fool cannot see that merit and good fortune are inseparably united.

Fortune, seeing that she could not make fools wise, has made them lucky.

Michel de Montaigne

Good fortune is a by-product, not something that can be demanded from life. We would do better to grieve less for the fortune we have never tasted and concentrate upon our own.

More have been ruined by their fortunes than have escaped ruin through their want of a fortune.

When fortune avoids us we feel it is because we are foolish or faint-hearted, but under the right circumstances every single one of us has within us the courage to face misfortune and always enough wisdom to offer friends and neighbors.

Praise without achievement is a meaningless narcotic. If you want to achieve nothing, do nothing.

Fortune takes careful courting. Woo her too intensely and she will edge away.

Fortunes are the fruits of a person's character. Found fortunes are rarely well suited to their owner.

He that waits upon fortune, is never sure of a dinner.

Benjamin Franklin

Like shoes, it is impossible to find a fortune to fit any person. Either they're too large and trip one up, or too small and one always feels the pinch.

It takes great courage to live decently a life that is driven by desires.

There can be no fortune until we are prepared to forget those things which are behind and reach forward toward those things which lie ahead.

A fortune made in haste is like a suit made in haste. Neither is likely to remain intact for long. Be ready to receive fortune when she calls for she does not visit often in a person's life and she'll fly out at the window if you are not.

Fortune favors the prepared mind.
Louis Pasteur

A great fortune depends on luck, a small one on diligence. Both depend on action.

We do not know what is
really good or bad fortune.
Jean Jacques Rousseau

**Fortune does not so
much change a person
as unmask them.**

The greatest fortune a person may have comes in the form of their friends. Friendship provides refuge, inspiration, comfort, support, and guidance. One need never know poverty when one has true friends.

The only fortune worth finding is an aim in life.

A red sky at night is said to be a shepherd's delight. A lucky omen—unless of course he is unlucky enough for it to signify that his house is burning down in the distance.

Do not seek your fortune by gambling—true wealth is to be found in aspirations and effort.

Welcome and embrace those moments of misfortune where life throws us upon our own resources. Times such as these develop our faculties and we become capable of things we never knew possible.

We are the men of intrinsic value, who can strike our fortunes out of ourselves, whose worth is independent of accidents in life, or revolutions in government: we have heads to get money, and hearts to spend it.

George Farquhar

Man's greatest misfortune is that he goes through life blissfully unaware of the immense power of his own free will. The wishes of God himself often never come to pass because man has chosen not to make them happen.

Throwing spilt salt over your left shoulder apparently knocks down the devil who is sitting there, which is good luck—but bad luck for the person standing behind you who gets salt in their eyes!

Only a fool drops a fortune in the shadows and then searches for it under the streetlamp because the light there is better.

The greatest test of good luck is this: when it comes does it provide the greatest results for the greatest number?

There is no action without expenditure of energy. Transfer of energy is the basis of human success and happiness.

Good which is unused is prone to turn to evil.

Wealth which comes to us by chance alone is more likely to weaken and destroy than bring happiness.

There is no science to luck and no formula for fortune.

One must become the architect of one's own character before one can become the architect of one's own fortune.

I would rather be adorned by beauty of character than jewels. Jewels are the gift of fortune, while character comes from within.

Plautus

Some people seem so intent upon constantly talking of their misfortunes that one begins to wonder whether secretly there is something in them that they find agreeable.

Better sometimes to bend a little and compromise than risk the snap of misfortune.

The person who can endure fortune and misfortune with equanimity, deprives misfortune of its power.

As a rock on the seashore he standeth firm,
and the dashing of the waves disturbeth him not.
He raiseth his head like a tower on a hill,
and the arrows of fortune drop at his feet.
In the instant of danger,
the courage of his heart sustaineth him;
and the steadiness of his mind beareth him out.

Akhenaton

**Fortune can take away our riches,
but never our courage to try again.**

**As for me, prizes are nothing.
My prize is my work.**

Katharine Hepburn

Making decisions is liberating, regardless of where they lead us, which is why so many of us seem so hell-bent upon walking headlong into disaster and misfortune.

Idleness never brought a person to the goal of their good fortune.

The ill pray for the good fortune of becoming well again. The moment their suffering is cured their satisfaction ebbs and they turn their sights on other desires.

Never admire another's fortune so much that you become dissatisfied with your own.

Envy is the rough nephew of justice and always comes down hard in the case of undeserved fortune.

Fortune and its sister misfortune are always exaggerated. Nobody is ever as content or as badly off as they would have us believe.

The man who comes up with a means for doing or producing almost anything better, faster, or more economically has his future and his fortune at his fingertips.

J. Paul Getty

Good and bad times are more to do with our changing moods than our changing fortunes.

Misfortunes that are accidents external to us can be endured, but we suffer greatly when our misfortune is brought about through our own faults.

Fortune is not blind. We are.

Nothing teaches us to rely less on luck than a lesson in misfortune. No venture is completely wasted that can result in our becoming a little bit wiser.

Be generous with your joy and show happiness over the good fortune of others.

They say that there is a pot of gold at the end of the rainbow. Nine times out of ten it is on the other side to the one we set out to find.

One likes people
much better when
they're battered down
by a prodigious siege
of misfortune than
when they triumph.

Virginia Woolf

Nothing is so
wretched or foolish
as to go through
life anticipating
misfortunes.

However many lucky words you read, however many you might speak, what good will they possibly do, if you are not prepared to act upon them?

Unlucky is he who was born with too great ambition, for ambition is a dish seasoned with disappointment, and the more of it he eats the hungrier he will become.

More go to ruined fortunes than are raised to fortune.

Fortune clearly befriends the bold.

It is an easy thing to put yourself down whenever you fail and to put others down when they succeed.

It is difficult to know which is worse to bear: a life that has experienced misfortune or a life that has been wasted fearing misfortunes that never came.

Calamities are of two kinds:
misfortune to ourselves,
and good fortune to others.

Ambrose Bierce

Whatever we are lucky or unlucky enough
to become one thing unites us all: we
share the common ground of having all
once been babies.

If the misfortunes of others hold
any lessons at all for us, let it be
to teach us caution.

The best portion of a good man's life,
His little, nameless, unremembered acts,
Of kindness and of love.

William Wordsworth

Look at those more fortunate than you
consider yourself to be and ask this question:
has their fortune sprung from their dedication
to work they enjoyed doing and which they
found profoundly absorbing?

**Whenever you pause to think
of how things might have been
and the chances you let slip by,
remember, they may also have
engulfed you in terrible misfortune.**

In human life there is constant change
of fortune; and it is unreasonable to
expect an exemption from the common
fate. Life itself decays, and all things are
daily changing.

Plutarch

**Change yourself and change
your fortunes.**

No human condition
is ever permanent.
So don't be too
overjoyed in good
fortune nor too scornful
in misfortune.

The quest for luck must be
undertaken with no regrets.
One must never look
behind—regret will only
serve to hold you back.

Without ambition one starts nothing.
Without work one finishes nothing.
The prize will not be sent to you.
You have to win it.

If one is to maximize on one's opportunities and chances one must begin to pay heed to one's lucky hunches.

People see privilege as good fortune.
We prize it over everything else,
whether it is holding first place in the
queue for a bowl of bad soup or being
made chief mourner at a funeral.

Just as treasures are uncovered from the earth, so virtue appears from good deeds, and wisdom appears from a pure and peaceful mind. To walk safely through the maze of human life, one needs the light of wisdom and the guidance of virtue.

Buddha

It's no good building a stairway to paradise if you're not prepared to climb it.

Shape your habits. Design them to achieve maximum happiness. What good is it sitting around waiting idly for good luck to come knocking at your door when it is clear that fortune's gates must be stormed and only the bravehearted will make the attack?

It is said that fortune knocks at every man's door at least once in a lifetime. The problem with this is that most of us appear to be out when it comes.

Fortune can, for her pleasure, fools advance, and toss them on the wheels of chance.

Juvenal

Good luck is but another name for tenacity of purpose.

Fortune cannot make fools wise; instead it makes them appear lucky.

Listen to people and you will hear that each is convinced there is good reason behind their good or bad luck. But despite what they may think, luck and fortune are not magic powers and fortune awaits those who grasp the fact that for every effect, there is a perfect cause.

It is the farmer plowing in the field alone, toiling unnoticed and uncheered, who wins the real prizes worth earning.

Our fortune depends less on luck than on diligence.

Success and failure are rarely commensurate with innate capacity. There is, in both, a considerable element of the unpredictable which we must take into account.

Fortune asks only that whatever we do, we don't always settle for the easy way.

I returned, and saw under the sun, that the race is not to the swift, nor the battle to the strong, neither yet bread to the wise, nor yet riches to men of understanding, nor yet favor to men of skill; but time and chance happeneth to them all.

Ecclesiastes 9:11

There is no luck to becoming the leader of others. One is only rewarded with the privileges of rank when one learns to selflessly avoid putting oneself before others. To some it is a privilege, to others it comes as a burden.

Approach all that you do with the desire to do it better than you have ever done it before, or better than it has ever been done before by others. This is the path to luck and fortune.

Let no one or anything stand between you and the difficult task. Let nothing deny you this rich chance to gain strength by adversity, confidence by mastery, and success by deserving it.

Half of those we would term as being geniuses would otherwise be perceived as being crazy people were it not for the fact that they happen to be more productive. Crazy people who are rich are perceived as being eccentric. Crazy people who are neither productive nor rich—well, they're just plain crazy.

The world was not built in a day. It took several.

There may be a certain amount of luck in getting a good job—but there's no luck involved in keeping it.

A heart well prepared for adversity in bad times hopes, and in good times fears, for a change in fortune.

Horace

Little minds are tamed and subdued by misfortune; great minds rise above misfortune.

It takes a special kind of person to be in possession of both good fortune and good sense.

Why is it that we insist upon always taking credit for the good and attributing everything bad to fortune?

The measure of any person is the way they bear up under misfortune.

The time will come when we shall realize that all we have paid has been nothing at all by comparison with the greatness of our prizes.

St. Teresa of Avila

**Where fortune is concerned
nothing is certain except that
action makes more than caution.**

Some find they can swim.
Others discover they drown.
The rest of us sit safely on the shore
and never risk getting our feet wet.

**When we learn to be accepting
of what happens to us, we take
the first step to overcoming the
consequences of our misfortune.**

Not everybody gets into the first team and not every flower is worthy of first prize, but taking part at any level brings its own little triumphs.

Mankind's dichotomy is that what he says he wants is rarely what he truly wants. Our fortunes lie in secret desires, in the dreams we never admit to.

Rarity is a magnet for good fortune. Exotic fruits in barren seasons and winter blooms even coyness draws.

When everyone is looking for gold,
It's a good time to be in the pick
and shovel business.

Mark Twain

Good fortune is a quality of
thought, a state of mind.

Where there is fortune, there is
boldness. Be gentle and you can
be bold.

The successful can always afford to be
indulgent toward their rivals.

Choices and Discoveries

The path to luck is twisted and awkward and difficult to navigate with any degree of certainty. It is riddled with discoveries which, each made, will make our onward journey more positive, optimistic, and rewarding.

Discover that two people can look at the exact same thing and see something totally different.

If we can find the passion within us to live a better life daily, it will fuel the energy we need to achieve it for a lifetime.

Luck and good fortune favor those who meet them halfway. It is therefore essential to motivate ourselves to find our trigger that allows us to jump into action and not to stop there but to go on and to gather momentum.

Our heart is the shaper of our thoughts, good and bad alike. It is the marriage of these thoughts and the choices we make which determine how we are perceived by the rest of the world. We are the makers and masters of our thoughts and our choices and, as such, the architects of our own characters.

Choice allows us to take stock, to analyze our life, and see what's missing from it. This empowers us to take control, creating the time to make choices and put them into action.

Every heart holds the potential to choose good or bad. When good becomes the majority choice the luckier our world becomes.

What makes lucky people stand out from an unlucky crowd is that along the way they seem to have realized that it takes years to build trust and only a moment to destroy it.

No person's luck can ever be built upon the foundation of cruelty to others.

There is nothing stopping us from seizing a moment and choosing from that magical instant to become lucky people, not for an hour or a day, but for all of what remains of our lives.

A noble and good character is not a thing of chance but a natural result of effort and right thinking.

The luckiest among us are those who can see clearly what it is that is stopping us from achieving our goals and who set about changing them.

Life is all about choice. It may not always seem that way but it comes down to each of us choosing whether we live in the country or dwell in the town, drink alcohol or nonalcoholic drinks, drive this or that make of car, and even how we might win or lose.

Life is more about choices than it is about luck.

Discover that it isn't always enough to be forgiven by others. Sometimes you have to be prepared to forgive yourself.

It is our own convictions which compel us: that is to say, choice compels choice.

One can either choose to be miserable or to motivate oneself out of being so. Either way, whatever must be done is always your choice.

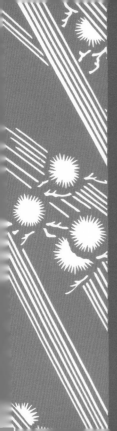

The light is there for all to see whether we choose to or not. When you have to make a choice and don't make it, that in itself is a choice.

The truly lucky are those of us who are able to stand up for our beliefs and do so without hurting the feelings of others.

The problem with choice is having the freedom to change one's mind. This inevitably results in us searching for some proof that our choice is okay and that there is no need for us to change our mind.

All of life is sacred, including our choices along the way. We become part of a choice to create an even better world when we choose to live our life consciously and within each moment.

Nobody in this world can have everything.
Even when we have nothing we still have choices.

Discover that people who don't even know you can change your life in a matter of hours.

Luck lies in making the correct choices, which is unlucky for those of us who find decision-making difficult.

We are all born with the gift of free choice, but choices should be made in the realization that we shall never be able to escape their consequences.

Choice is often the greatest difficulty we face in life. The lucky seem to get past this; the unlucky wait and see.

Discover that even when you think you have nothing left to give, when a friend or loved one cries out to you, you will always somehow find the strength to help.

One of the great paradoxes of life is that the more equally inviting two alternatives appear to us, the harder it becomes for us to choose between them.

Discover that just because two people argue, it doesn't mean they don't love or care for each other, and just because they don't argue with each other doesn't mean that they do.

Choice empowers us and tempts luck to visit us.

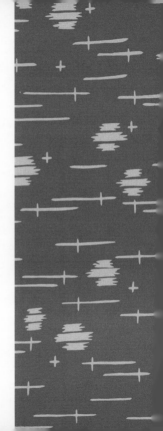

Discover that no matter how good a friend or how close a loved one, they are inevitably going to hurt you every once in a while; if you can move ahead with this knowledge you can and will forgive them as and when it occurs.

If you believe yourself to be indecisive, consider this: by choosing not to make a decision you have made a choice.

Avoid choosing to pursue a life whose sole purpose is financial abundance and you will avoid living a troubled life.

Make your choice for the pleasure of making it. No right choice need ever be painful if we can understand why it was made.

It is the thought of luck
not luck itself that usually
urges us on. Only one
brings pleasure.

Love comes to us whether we want it or not. It is not a question of choice but a matter of fate.

I am not an adventurer by choice but by fate.

Vincent van Gogh

Discover that when someone doesn't love you the way you would wish them to, it does not mean that they don't love you with everything they've got.

Our choices, once made, seal our fate.

Discover that you cannot make somebody love you. You can, however, choose to become someone who can be loved and leave the rest to them.

Discover that every relationship begins with enthusiasm and verve but initial passion eventually fades and some of us are lucky enough to have something there to take its place.

A person's philosophy is best expressed through their choices.

Maturity has nothing to do with how many candles are on your birthday cake and everything to do with your choice of experiences and what lessons you've chosen to carry away from them.

We should always try to make the best possible choices we can if we wish to become the best people we can possibly be.

Our choices shape our lives and we shape our choices so ultimately we must take full responsibility. The luckless always have someone or something else to blame.

Look closely at your choices and pick the best one, the one you believe in, and back it with all your heart but perhaps not with all of your money!

You should never tell any person, especially a child, that their dreams are unlikely or mere fantasy. Not only is it humiliating but it would be a terrible waste to mankind if they chose to believe it.

There is no sacrifice: only choices to make.

At any given moment in any person's life, there is always a choice.

There are always two choices, two paths to take. One is always easier and more tempting, but beware—that may be all it has to offer.

Realize that no matter the depths of your despair, the world doesn't stop for your grief.

Our primary choices in life are to choose to accept things as they are or to choose to accept responsibility for changing them.

Every choice has a result. The rub is that it may not always be the desired result.

A horseshoe, hung upright above the doorway, is considered to bring good luck to a home. Unless, of course, you are unlucky enough to walk under one that has not been hung correctly and it falls on your head!

Whatever the circumstances, aim to be positive in your behavior and responses and your choices will also become more positive.

Well-made choices are wonderful contributors to our well-being.

Our choices determine how we will experience our life.

It's choice, not chance, that determines one's destiny. A life spent waiting for it is a life wasted.

Discover that the credentials hanging on the wall do not make a person a decent human being.

To be successful one must realize
before it's too late that things do not
run on luck alone, but by the laws
of cause and effect we are all the
beginning, we are all the end, not just
a link in the chain of time.

We cannot turn around our luck until
we are able to live in tranquil harmony
with that which is considered unlucky.
Until then, we will not be free of fear.

The things a man has to have are hope and confidence in himself against odds, and sometimes he needs somebody, his pal or his mother or his wife or God, to give him that confidence.

He's got to have some inner standards worth fighting for or there won't be any way to bring him into conflict. And he must be ready to choose death before dishonor without making too much song and dance about it. That's all there is to it.

Clark Gable

Strangely, it is quite often people we are not related to who, if we choose to accept it, show us love and care in our hour of need; and it is they who rekindle our trust in people.

A person's self is something that is in a continual state of formation through an entire lifetime. We form it through our choices and actions.

Give your garden the freedom of choice to express itself and it will reward you with a fine display of weeds and natural chaos. Give it no choice but to grow those things that you plant and you stand a chance of being the lucky winner of a prize for best-kept garden. It comes down to a matter of choosing which is the better prize.

Your life-changing moment will arrive when you accept that you have within you the power of choice.

Discover that you can get by on charm for, at most, several minutes. After that, you had better be sure that you know something.

When we acknowledge our freedom of choice, we take the first step toward unleashing our own personal power and can expect, if we believe in ourselves and take positive action, to start seeing some results that will amaze others and ourselves.

Discover that we don't have to change friends. If we can bring ourselves round to understanding that friends change when we exercise our power of choice and free ourselves from the dictates of others, we can begin to realize our personal goals; and those of us in relationships will discover that mutual goals are achievable and that our choices can bring us closer together.

Ignore your personal power to make choices and you will miss out on much good luck in life.

Discover that often the people we care most about in life are taken from us far too soon.

If, like countless others around the world, you want to change your life for the better, don't lose the moment—act on it and make your choice.

Choice is the freedom to turn our dreams into reality.

Sometimes the people you expect to kick you when you're down will be the ones who help you up.

We all have it within us to create for ourselves an exceptional quality of life by developing our independence through simply adopting a psychology which embraces and nurtures our freedom to make choices.

When we feel cut off from choice we feel at our unluckiest and that we are no longer in control of our lives or our emotions.

We tend to stand back and look on in awe at high achievers from the sidelines when we should be taking action, if only in an attempt to increase our own energy. If we can achieve that, we will begin to produce results faster than we had ever imagined possible and, before long, we can become high achievers ourselves.

There is no purpose to a life that is lived with no results in mind.

We need to cut free and allow ourselves to sail with the wind and the tides on a sea of "can do."

The negative mind is like an anchor bedding us to the ocean floor with its limiting beliefs.

The luckiest people alive were just like you until they rearranged their game of life, not only to achieve their goals, but to go about it in a manner that allows them to enjoy the process.

It takes just as much effort to hold you to the lowest possible standards as it would to hold yourself up to the highest possible standards. Choose well.

No matter how much you go through life caring for others there will inevitably be those who will not reciprocate. We like to tell our friends and colleagues to depend on us, to lean on us when they need help, to call on us for support in their quests but often we are guilty ourselves of not turning to and utilizing our peer groups in our own quests.

Choice allows us to create special relationships with others that are longlasting and fulfilling.

True friendship continues to grow, even over the longest distance. The same is true of love. Choose to turn your back on these and you will end up counting your losses.

Best friends can do anything together or nothing at all together and have the best of times either way.

We are lucky if we are able to understand the true nature of our relationships—exactly what they are and just why it is we need them. Lack of such understanding only serves to create conflict in any relationship and we spend our time and energy trying to solve things we cannot comprehend.

Before making any choice it is a good thing to ask oneself silently and calmly what it is we really want from the choice we are about to make.

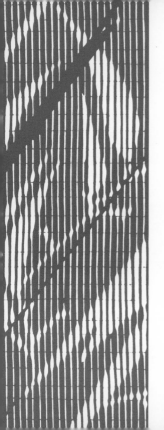

The most important choice we can all make is to choose to create understanding and meaningful relationships, beginning with ourselves. This done, we have embarked on a life where it will become possible to make any relationship work.

If one knows exactly what one wishes to get out of any relationship, one can then base one's choices upon achieving this aim. These will not always be simple or obvious, but will end up being the right ones.

Discover that money is always a bad way of keeping score.

Make choices that will free you to expand your level of fulfillment in all that you do.

How many of us go through our lives bottling up our emotions and passions? We waste this gift of life and time by spending our energies upon hiding them away when surely we can only ever hope to be fully alive by unleashing even the deepest of them.

If your choice is to become successful, then choose successful role models. For success is a treacherous terrain far too dangerous to enter without a guide. Learn from their mistakes; learn from their choices.

Within us there is an abundance of energy waiting for us to choose to release it. In doing so we stimulate a new vitality in our life, which can have marvellously positive effects upon our health and well-being.

It's not so much "what" we have in our lives as "who" we have that counts.

With choice and an understanding of our own emotions we open an entirely new box of tricks. With such understanding we discover how even our negative emotions can serve us well.

It is an unlucky world where everything that is undertaken in it is done in the hope of bringing someone credit or reward.

Daily we are faced with the choice of going on as we are or of changing things, perhaps in our diet or lifestyle, that could help us to restore our lives, our shape, or our energy.

With understanding of the power of personal choice we come to know when it is best to follow our emotions and when it would be better for us to ignore them.

Those who stand among us in a perpetual state of imbalance are the ones who find it impossible to make their minds up. There is only one way forward, which is to risk making a choice! With luck, our choice will be the right one. If not, then at least the cycle will have been broken and one can then go on to make new and better informed decisions to get life back on course.

Each of us also carries within us the potential for our own pain and disease, which we unwittingly unleash by making regrettable decisions. It is therefore up to us to regain control. We cannot rewind time or change things back to the way they were, but we can learn from it and endeavor to steer toward our future with greater care.

Discover that heroes are people who do nothing more than what has to be done when it needs to be done, regardless of the consequences.

The most important investment decision any person can make is to invest in himself. This is the foundation block for all choice.

Discover that you should never compare yourself to the best that others have to offer or you will always fall short of the mark.

The thing that keeps many of us from wealth is mankind's inherent nature for falling into the same traps over and over again.

It only takes an instant to create a heartache that lasts for a lifetime.

Develop in yourself the ability to take conscious control of how you think, how you feel, and perhaps most importantly, how you choose to behave.

Choose to view life as a journey and not a destination and you will immediately begin to appreciate that all things are possible, that life is not directionless, and that there are discoveries to be made daily, all through our freedom of choice.

In general it takes more than a lifetime to become the person we all want to be.

Our background and circumstances may have influenced who we are, but we are responsible for who we become.

Each of us has been granted the gift of a life and each life has its own unique purpose. When we discover what that purpose is (and the clues to this lie in the choices we make along the way), we can set about living it purposefully.

Make each parting special and leave loved ones with loving words. It may be the last time we ever see them.

Choose the words you utter with care for people will hear them and be influenced by them for good or ill. This can be lucky or unlucky for us.

Learn that it is usually possible to keep going beyond the point where you think you can't.

Life is filled with challenges, some designed to defeat us, some to subdue us. But all are there to be conquered and can be through the power of our decisions and choices.

Discover that we are responsible for what we do, no matter how we feel, win or lose.

The greatest choice you can make is to create time for you and to use it to prepare your mind, body, and spirit for the journey of a lifetime.

Either control your attitude or it will soon control you.

When we learn to harness the power of decision we have it within us to turn almost any dream we have into a reality.

You should never be too eager to discover a secret. It could just change your luck forever either way.

An unfocused life is like listening to a half-tuned radio, but we can tune ourselves in to those things we wish for most in every area of our lives by filling our empty and otherwise wasteful moments with the setting of clearly defined goals.

To find luck and fortune you must first learn to understand the driving force behind all human behavior and the needs that control what we think, what we feel, and what we do.

To get better results we need to begin by changing ourselves. We must be prepared to change our patterns of thinking and of behaving, and to adapt our feelings.

Luck
and the
Gambler

To a gamester nothing is sacred except Lady Luck herself.

The dice of Zeus always fall luckily.
Sophocles

Gamblers are locked in a perpetual state of being excited even when they are locked in a perpetual state of losing.

Nobody has much time for a losing gambler, but show them a winner and they congregate like moths around the candle, hoping some of the luck will rub off.

Some gamble with their very souls and when they lose, feel no more emotion than they would if they had mislaid their car keys.

If you gain,
you gain all;
if you lose, you
lose nothing.
Wager then,
without
hesitation, that
He exists.

Blaise Pascal

Opportunities don't always just come along. One has to dig them out and this often means taking chances, following our curiosity, and sometimes, gambling is our only method of taking advantage of them when we unearth them.

The advice is don't gamble. The noble face of gambling is the stock market where fortunes are won and lost daily.

The world is a casino and none shall know until the end of their days here exactly what they have lost or won.

One is frowned upon for risking one's shirt on such and such a horse or the big game, yet people are positively thrilled at the prospect of you gambling away your entire life and fortune on getting married to someone you barely know.

If you seek a guaranteed income from following the horses, you would do better to do it with a broom and a shovel.

The gambler believes wholeheartedly in luck. His perception of his Creator must be of someone locked in an eternal game of dice with the universe as the stake.

Gambling combines man's playful curiosity and his desire to discover his fate.

Nothing cures a person of their delusions and daydreams like an hour or so spent locked in a losing streak.

A shark is someone who believes that suckers are unlucky with money and has the skill to relieve them of it.

Gambling is any behavior which involves risking money or anything that has value on the outcome of an event in which the outcome is partially or entirely dependent upon chance.

If you want to make everybody happy play poker badly.

The odds are only ever in our favor when we are prepared to do absolutely everything it is necessary for us to do.

If you really want to win there is no easy path. It takes courage, determination, and a bit of self-control.

Gambling eliminates strikes. People need to work in order to have money to bet.

In the cemetery of a gambling town a headstone reads, "Not dead…just sleeping" under which is chalked: "I'll bet $100 you're dead!"

The calmest person in the world is the one who has four aces and a heap of faith.

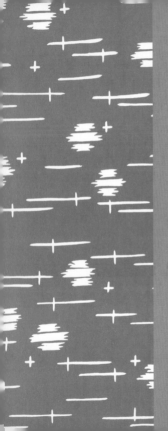

Nothing is a sure
thing, for all things
depend on a
complex chain of
unseen chances.
Even the cheat who
stacks the odds in
his favor can never
be certain of
winning.

The Internet is the ideal playroom for the idle player.

If you want to feel lucky and still play roulette, better to be the owner of the table.

While there still exist bets to be won gambling will continue. It is inherent in nature and particularly in human nature.

You can usually bet safely that those who protest loudest against relationships already have someone in mind that they'd like to hook up with.

It takes ambition and a little luck to start anything and determination to finish it.

Luck is a global commodity: on a dollar for dollar basis nothing is more popular today than gambling.

The gambling known as business looks with severe disfavor on the business known as gambling.

Ambrose Bierce

The prayer of the gambler is in the main: "Please let me break even today, for I need the money!"

Whether you wager on the existence of black holes, or that a person might walk around the world and not be recognized, or bet on when the ice might break on an Alaskan river, the only luck you can depend upon is either your prior knowledge of facts, the probability of being correct, or your best guess at the time.

Every successful political leader
has within them a gambler's
instinct. Every religious leader
carries the belief that they are
on to a sure thing.

Prizes are seldom freely sent to us. They must be won.

When the flowers we nurse have faded away, the grass we trample upon continues to flourish.

Put your money where your mouth is and take action.

One should not measure a person's success upon their accomplishments but by their courage to carry on even against overwhelming odds.

It is not uncommon to bet on a winning horse. What is uncommon is to ever bet enough on the winning horse.

One may take a gamble without financial risk, usually through engaging in any high-risk behavior in which actions or decisions are made despite incomplete knowledge.

Gambling offers a world of color, fancy, excitement, and wonder: a potentially ruinous combination.

The luckiest throw of the dice one can make is out of the window into the river.

Gambling is often viewed as evil, perhaps because it is so very universal an urge and so pleasurable a practice.

In a bet there is a fool and a thief.

Proverb

It is lucky to be gifted with the talent to do card tricks, but foolish to perform them for those you play poker with.

One imagines that the swiftest will win the race and that the strongest will win the battle, but it is not always so, although these are the safest bets.

Gambling is viewed as unsociable and gamblers are perceived as dishonest, possibly because betting is at base about the transference of property without toil or productivity.

The only way to beat the roulette table is to knock out the croupier and steal the money.

Gambling for many people is merely a form of recreation, but like any behavior which stimulates brain chemistry, it can easily become a psychologically addictive and harmful behavior.

Do not expect to gain anything from nature or religion through gambling.

The greatest opportunity one has to discover just how cruel luck can be is when one borrows money to wager on a bet.

With every turn of the card, every race run, each cast of the dice, the gambler is reinvented. Ambition and desire in anything else may wane, but show the gambler any form of game and it will sustain his interest a dozen times longer than anything else.

Luck never made a man wise.

Seneca

Do not seek fortune at the gaming table for she is elsewhere in the company of industry.

All life is a lottery: gaming at its grandest scale of winning and losing where the biggest stake is life itself.

One of the unluckiest things that can happen to anyone at an early age is to win a bet on a horse.

Italians come to ruin most generally in three ways, women, gambling, and farming. My family chose the slowest one.

Pope John XXIII

The only thing that can beat a Royal Flush is divine intervention or a loaded gun.

Gambling is the child of avarice and the parent of despair. No amount of luck will ever make this relationship a fulfilling one.

The degenerate gambler gambles for the sake of gambling like the mercenary who will lay down his life for the sake of battle. There are no winners and no losers here, only corpses, living and dead.

The odds of coming through life unscathed are 6 to 5 against.

Gambling is the promise of something for nothing rather in the way property performs for the rich. This is why it is so seductive to those who can little afford to do it.

Gambling is the door that leads to avarice, iniquity, and mischief.

If you must play, decide upon three things at the start: the rules of the game, the stakes, and the quitting time.

Chinese proverb

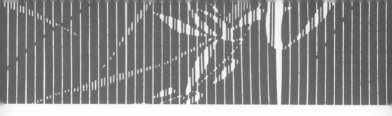

The only chance that games of chance offer is usually the chance to lose. If one wants to narrow the odds and still gamble then it would be better to stick to blackjack where winning is not unheard of.

When asked about his mother's visit to Las Vegas the weekend before she died, President Clinton is quoted as saying: "She got to go to heaven four days early."

The greatest hope we can have for our offspring if they should be unfortunate enough to have in them the gambling instinct gene, is that they also possess a good sense of probabilities.

It is the nature of men and women to find greater satisfaction in the discovery of a small amount of money lying in the street than all the money they earned through honest toil. The money won at cards or in the stock market generates this same warm feeling in their hearts.

If you want to double your money in an instant and not risk losing any of it then take out a banknote, fold it in half, and put it back in your pocket.

Anyone who believes they are a winner and that they are always lucky is either a liar, a fool, or a cheat.

The casino is the larder and the slot machines the mousetraps, the punters are the mice and the promise of prizes is the bait.

If I lose today, I can look forward to winning tomorrow, and if I win today, I can expect to lose tomorrow. A sure thing is no fun.

Chico Marx

Fortune truly helps those who are of good judgment.

Euripides

When your opponent's sittin' there holdin' all the aces, there's only one thing to do: kick over the table.

Dean Martin

When one considers risk statistically, the world is inhabited mainly by gamblers.

The first big gamble took place in the Garden of Eden.

I used to be a heavy gambler. But now I just make mental bets. That's how I lost my mind.

Steve Allen

Nothing lights the gambler's fuse more than those four little words: "It cannot be done."

The gambler can see an entire world in a pair of dice, and a future in a deck of cards. Armed with these weapons, win or lose, he'll still feel lucky.

There are three types of punters who enter casinos: the idle rich with nothing to lose; the professional gamblers who have studied the games well; and all the rest who fall into the category of victims.

Even as I approach the gambling hall, as soon as I hear, two rooms away, the jingle of money poured out on the table, I almost go into convulsions.

Fyodor Dostoevsky

Atheists and moralists are not unalike. When it comes to religion or gambling, they judge each by its excesses.

No wife can endure a gambling husband unless he is a steady winner.

Lord Dewar

Nothing tests a person's faith quite as intensely as a desperate gambler on a losing streak.

If you don't try your luck, you can't know Fortune's potential.

The thing that seems to go against any belief or understanding of luck is the way that the majority of players who go into casinos don't have a clue how to play.

The most fulfilling way to gamble is with a garden spade and a packet of seeds.

A person does not seek luck;
luck seeks the person.

Turkish proverb

There are many victories worse than a defeat.

Mankind lives tethered to his conditioning and training and ends up believing that the odds are too heavy against him to cut himself loose of these ties and risk anything new.

Those who know how will always have employment. Those who know how and why will always be their boss.

With a good grasp of principles and probabilities, a person may choose their own methods, but method that ignores these leads only to trouble.

One should always play fair when one has the winning cards.

Oscar Wilde

One somehow feels that there is great honor in trying and failing. It is the loser's safety net.

Winning is a meaningless narcotic and nothing soothes the ego more than the feeling that you are lucky.

The greatest prize comes through toiling, unaided and alone.

It is the striving to win that brings the greatest joy and the prize itself is secondary.

There are two great pleasures in gambling: that of winning and that of losing.

French proverb

The best odds anyone can be offered is to begin anything with an even break.

The main thing that unites most gamblers is their inability to know when to quit. Luck is mainly about common sense—the ability to understand that it is wise to quit when you are ahead.

The excitement felt when placing a bet is equal to the amount one might win multiplied by the probability of winning it.

A lifetime is the biggest gamble of all. If one were to study its odds, chances are nobody would ever bet on it.

A dealer told a card player to stop cheating. "I'm not cheating!" exclaimed the player. To which the dealer replied: "But you're not playing the hand I dealt you."

Even in a one-horse race there is never the certainty that a horse will finish.

At that point I ought to have gone away, but a strange sensation rose up in me, a sort of defiance of fate, a desire to challenge it, to put out my tongue at it. I laid down the largest stake allowed—four thousand gulden—and lost it. Then, getting hot, I pulled out all I had left, staked it on the same number, and lost again, after which I walked away from the table as though I were stunned. I could not even grasp what had happened to me.

Fyodor Dostoevsky

The only person who has any right to feel comfortable at the gaming table is a rich gambler with nothing to lose.

Baccarat is a game whereby the croupier gathers in money with a flexible sculling oar, then rakes it home. If I could have borrowed his oar I would have stayed.

Mark Twain

Unlucky is the innumerate person who stumbles upon a field of four-leaf clovers.

The smarter one plays anything, the luckier one is.

Nothing is more capable of corrupting a person's disposition than gaming.

A true gambler will never let winning or losing affect him emotionally. When it does, he should walk away and live to play another day.

Every person dies sooner or later and most would rather lose the bet than lay odds on their own early demise.

You should never bet against anything in science at odds of more than about 10^{12} to 1.

Ernest Rutherford

Gambling is a form of madness where reason crosses swords with risk.

Those who abstain from gaming and say they do not envy the winning millionaire are gambling themselves on the odds that they wouldn't enjoy trading places if offered the chance.

Chicolini: My dog—believe me, he's some smart dog. You know he went with Admiral Byrd to the Pole.

Firefly: I'll bet the dog got to the pole first.

Duck Soup **(1933)**

It seems to have been evolved into man's nature that he rise up from all fours onto his own two feet to walk headlong into risky situations.

When one truly believes in what one does then it is worth taking the calculated risk and summoning up the courage to bet on one's ideas.

No matter our views on gambling, when money is won it always seems twice as sweet as money earned.

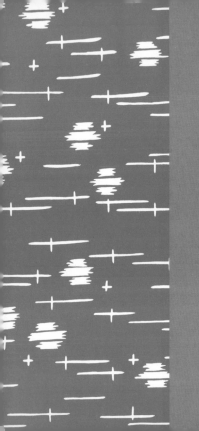

If diving from a bridge into a river, it would be wise to know first if the water is deep and free of submerged rocks, otherwise one must be either mad or certain of one's luck.

I have always wagered
against God and I regard
the little that I have won
in this world as simply
the outcome of this bet.
However paltry may have
been the stake (my life) I
am conscious of having
won to the full.

André Breton

When two people have opposing views of what is true or forthcoming, yet each remains certain on their part, then chances are, provided it will eventually become possible to determine who was actually right, that they will enter into a token bet with each other as to the outcome. Winning and one-upmanship will be the driving force, not profit.

The single most
popular gambling
strategy that is
used worldwide
is guesswork.

Imagine having the mind of a compulsive gambler. Why, he couldn't even walk to the end of the street and see two birds sitting on a fence without making a silent wager to himself on which one would be the first to fly away.

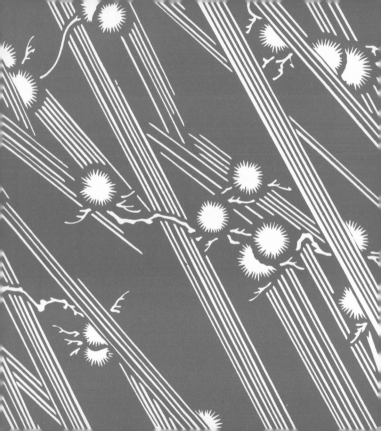

The Part
Chance
Plays

Whereas luck relies heavily upon chance, a person's labors rely upon their character.

Do not fool yourself that the smiles of fortune have not been earned. Although luck may rely upon chance, luck itself is not chance.

Chances taken equal toil.

Opinions survive only if one has the chance to fight for them.

Chance itself is not enough. It requires our preparedness—luck will come when we have readied ourselves for the chance.

The older and wiser among us see youth as the luckiest time of life, for it is from the radiance and innocence of youth that the future will always spring.

If you have the good sense to recognize an opportunity and possess the ability to take advantage of it, then you have luck.

He who can smile at his breaks and grab hold of chances will always get on.

Luck should never be left entirely up to chance. One must help by creating opportunity, and develop the ability to recognize it when it is there. Then, one must be able to grab it when it comes.

**You cannot test your luck
if you don't bother to show up.**

Luck can be extremely predictable...
The less active you are and fewer chances you
take, the less luck will show you its face. Make
the effort, take the chances, and become more
active, and luck will follow you around.

**It is foolish to dream of freedom
when there always exists the chance
to fight for it.**

Mankind's golden opportunities constantly seem to elude him because of a fundamental misunderstanding which leads him to seek these things outside of himself, when all along they exist within all of us.

Leadership is not attained by chance or through mere indulgence. It demands careful preparation, great trust, and a spirit of loyalty.

Rely on others, or upon chance or luck, and opportunities will be missed. Seek opportunity from within yourself and these things will come to you.

Each generation inherits from the previous one this Planet Earth. It is not a matter of chance or luck. Our debt for this is payable in one way only and that is in emulating their best ideals for a safe, clean, and wholesome world.

Luck owes as much to accident as it does to chance and opportunity.

Chance is the providence of every adventurer.

Good health is not merely a matter of luck. We all have the chance to be loyal to ourselves by conserving our physical well-being, our strength, and vigor.

Luck depends upon taking chances. There is so little luck around today because in the realistic practical world, the wise have been taught to avoid speculation.

Take your chances without fear of failure, just as the child takes its first breath outside the womb and goes on to take its first steps in life.

Achievement cannot be left to chance and luck. When a person loves what it is they do, they may accomplish a great many things regularly—to wait for chance, luck, or opportunity would result in little or no achievement.

Chance fights ever on the side of the prudent.

Is it by luck or design that everything classical appears to be through necessity while things modern appear capricious and to have come about by mere chance?

Do not confuse chance with choice. It is chance that makes our parents, but choice that makes our friends.

Chance is there for everyone equally.
Nobody owes anybody anything
but everyone is entitled to their chance.

**In determining right from wrong,
exercise restraint for, given a
chance, right will always appear.**

Chance is the pseudonym
God uses when He does not
want to sign His name.

Anatole France

In the hands of the wise, chance is soon turned into good fortune.

All we are saying is give peace a chance.

John Lennon

If one wishes to go through life doing few things badly, then it would be better not to trust in chance. The only sadness in this is that one will inevitably go through life doing very few things at all.

All life is based upon guesses.
To survive one must make one's best guess after best guess and hope that one is right. With luck one may actually get somewhere and given half a chance, may even live to a ripe old age.

Chance comes just as a beautiful day comes and disappears with the setting of the sun.

All life is chance—we do not ask for it to begin and we do not ask for it to end.

Grieving offers us the chance to grow, the chance to develop into gentler human beings, the chance to become somehow greater for our pain, and the greatest chance of all—to come through it richer and better for the experience.

Study and prepare and with luck, perhaps your chance will come.

Nothing that is of importance should be left to chance.

Those who enter into anything believing it may not work or anxious that it might fail will be surpassed by those who light their rocket with the fuse of a 1% chance of success.

Chance is the governor of disaster. It is a bringer of happiness but rarely of peace.

The future of the world cannot be left to luck or mere chance. It requires men and women of unimpeachable character to make popular the right ideals.

Chance is an adventure. If certainty is your desire then you must buy every raffle ticket and await the inevitable.

In order to be successful one must either have a chance or take one.

Court chance and she shall favor you.

One good chance is all one needs.

Chance favors the prepared mind.
To everyone else it comes in the form
of accidents.

**Life is an incredible journey and owes
as much to random chance as it does
to logic and reason.**

The truly lucky person in this world
is the one who is prepared to give
others a chance.

One must never dwell upon what might have been, for this is the place of sadness. Chances that have slipped by will never return again and we must let them go to travel on with new and better awareness.

When we take chances, of course we stand to lose. But is it not also true that without taking chances nothing stands a chance of ever changing for the better.

In every person's lifetime things occur by mere chance which we would never have dared to hope for.

Charity is good luck received at times of hope. It is the chance lucky receipt of money to be placed toward positive action, to answer the needy prayers of others and provide hope, while gambling is the giving of money for the mere hope of receiving good luck by chance.

Coincidences are the nearest thing there are to little miracles.

Opportunities are chances that are seen as being lucky but consider the lure of the seductress Temptation. She always offers second chances.

Every chance taken is another chance to win and at the same time, another chance to lose.

Fat chance and slim chance are twin sisters, each determined to repel the other's advances.

Sometimes our hour of suffering is the turning hour of our life. It is the hour to be and the hour to do— an opportunity not to be missed.

If we take chances, we stand a likelihood of losing. But without participating, how can we ever hope to win? To become lucky one must be aware of the possibility of losing, and be prepared to accept one's losses. By taking small chances, we risk only small losses and stand to make potential larger gains.

Luck is developing the ability to avoid being hindered and recognizing when to let go.

Do not waste your sympathy on me because I have to work. The greatest prize that life offers is the chance to be able to work hard at something that is worth doing.

The first time Adam had a chance, he laid the blame on a woman.

Nancy Astor

Luck requires total effort. If the odds appear to be stacked against you, you must never quit or stop trying. Only then will you retain your chance to win through.

It is considered bad luck to light three cigarettes with the same match but the truth of this myth comes not from superstition but trench warfare in WWI when snipers would take careful aim and fire a fateful bullet at the third target.

Opportunity rarely if ever knocks twice, and our fate is sealed by the choices we take.

One spends one's life torn between one's own firm resolve and the temptations of chance, destiny, and fate.

Before complaining about growing old, consider those who never got the chance.

Hard work never killed anybody, but many of us figure: "Why should I take the chance?"

**The greatest chance
we take is to put off
until tomorrow those
things we could do
today in an unclouded
yet unfounded
probability that
tomorrow will come.**

Read the best books
first or you may not
have a chance to
read them all.
                Henry David Thoreau

Every single one of us living today is unique, each with a life to live that will be filled with chances and momentous choices and it is our choices that make or mar not only our own life, but the life of our communities and the life of the world.

Keep your eye always on the main chance and don't allow yourself to be distracted by the smallest thing.

If one goes through life fearing ridicule, hurt, embarrassment, or failure, then one goes through life never taking any chances at all.

If one wants to narrow the odds then life can always be viewed as having a fifty percent chance of anything— either it happens or it doesn't.

We live in a world of growing equal opportunities, which means that soon everyone will have an equal chance at being equally incompetent.

Everybody feels they deserve a second chance but not necessarily on the same terms.

All life is filled with chance.
To go far one must be prepared and willing to
be daring and to do—and to take a chance.

**All human actions are driven by causes
whether by chance, nature, compulsion,
habit, reason, passion, or desire.**

Leadership is driven by fear not luck—the
fear that, given half a chance, people will
retaliate and do as they have been done by.

Be careful how you use your first chance,
for none of us get second chances in this life.
We of course get many new and different
chances but never a second chance under
the same set of circumstances.

Chance helps those who help themselves.

Throughout history luck has decreed that most of mankind shall abhor determinism while maintaining a vibrant intolerance of chance.

Some shy away from hard work, believing it leads nowhere without a measure of good luck. Those who make it in this world tend to be the ones who take the chance that they can do so on hard work alone.

**Adventure is the road to good fortune
and it is paved with chance.
Expect anything along the way.**

It is easy to put everything down to chance or
accident. By doing so we merely illustrate our
ignorance of some real and immediate cause.

**The destiny of the world at any given time
depends not upon luck but the opinions
and actions of its populace—particularly
its youth. It is up to each of us to fight for
equality and brotherhood and remove all
chances that any person, anywhere, is
made to feel unwanted.**

Luck is about knowing how to respond to chance. The same chance that arises to steal a million offers the opportunity not to steal and to avoid being caught and branded a criminal for the rest of your life.

Even the dishonest among us are sometimes not so purely by chance.

Show willingness and chances will come.

Much of what exists today came about despite the opinion that these things were possibly too wacky for the general public to accept.

Youth, conviction, and courage is a combination potentially capable of determining the kind of world we shall live in.

Ardor and diligence are the keys that unlock the doors behind which lie the chances to learn.

Life is filled with chances:
the chance to love,
the chance to work,
the chance to play,
and the chance to look up at the stars
and dream.

Chance is powerful. Cast your hook
in the pool where you least expect it,
and chances are there will be a fish.

If, in an allotted time, you don't complete
half the task by the midway point,
chances are you'll end up leaving the
rest of the task undone.

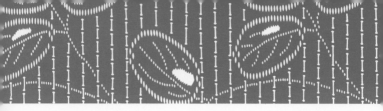

Hard work is not a guarantee of success but without it we don't stand a chance.

Lucky people are just as aware as unlucky people of the possibility of losing.

Anything played with confidence stands a good chance of convincing others—this is true from politics to poker.

If there's the slightest chance you'll wish you'd been there or done something, then go or do it, or you will certainly miss out.

We are not, as many believe, mere puppets controlled by chance or fate. Look at invention and look at art—every stroke of the brush, every push of a button should serve to demolish such a theory.

A person's destiny is not a matter of chance, it is a matter of choice. Our destiny is not something to wish for but rather something to strive to attain.

None of us will be offered second chances to make a good first impression.

One must be willing to accept small losses if one wants to be in the position of making large gains.

If one wants to be noticed, consider all that you say and do and aim for those things that there's a good chance nobody's seen or heard before.

Travel your life with confidence and willingness and tell the world with veracity everything you heard and saw. Chances are that what you have to say will be greatly valued by many others.

Some believe that there is no such thing as chance and that even the slightest accident that befalls us springs from the deepest source of our destiny.

It is painfully frustrating that whenever we do something worthy of merit the world will accuse us of stealing the idea—or worse, will believe that it was by chance.

One's greatest chance for happiness comes not by heeding only to the voices of others, but to occasionally paying heed to one's own.

Time is luck. Without time we'd have no opportunity to seek solutions, find answers to our questions, or consider ideas.

When chances arise and we resort to mere expedients and tricks then the opportunity is lost.

Everybody might have a chance to be pretty good at what they do.

It's very lucky to meet a chimney sweep by chance. Make a wish when you see one, and it is said that your wish will come true.

Extra time gives us more chances—it gives some the chance to complete the task, and others the chance to make the same mistakes.

We all have the equality of chance to do the most ridiculous things imaginable with our lives—that is the nature of democracy.

Chance plays a role in almost everything. It is the frustrating element that makes it possible for the bravest to be felled by the most cowardly on the battlefield.

A recipe for happiness: plan your days well and leave your nights open to chance.

A person's lifetime is a disorientating place to reside…One must occasionally give oneself the chance of a break or a vacation if one is to have the chance to regain one's sense of direction.

Failure is the condiment that gives success its flavor.

Truman Capote

When offered the chance of some help from another, to refuse would deprive both the giver and the receiver of the lucky chance to be helped and to be helpful.

If one is to place one's trust in chance, one must be prepared to abide by the rules of chance.

Truth often doesn't stand a chance
where a good lie has gained a hold.

**Love is designed only for those of us
who are fool enough and wise enough
to take our chances with it.**

Failure is not something we should worry
about. If you must worry, then let it be
about all the chances that are missed
because of not even trying.

**Freedom offers those fortunate enough
to be granted it the chance to be better.**

Leave the things that need doing to chance and chances are they'll never get done.

He is a charlatan who condemns corruption mainly because he has not been lucky enough to have been invited to participate in it himself.

It is bad luck to interfere with nature. She knows her business better than we do and, given a chance, she will outdo us every time.

Find within you your confidence in yourself—important decisions should never be left to chance alone.

The prepared stargazer who knows what he's looking for is more likely to be favored by chance than an unprepared bystander.

Opportunity

Drive the tension out from your life and seek to develop a more relaxed approach to what you do. This includes opening yourself up to new possibilities and new experiences—new, exciting, and lucky opportunities will arise.

When you're surrounded by a heap of troubles you can either put on some very tight shoes to take your mind off them or contemplate the "why" that underpins them. Use this as an opportunity to understand, not to be overwhelmed.

Resist the temptation to diminish your expectations of yourself. Pressure and rising tension can always be turned into positive energy.

A man with Alzheimer's once said that the nice part about it was that whenever he didn't know what he was doing, there was always some other loving soul who did.

Make the iron hot by striking it.
Oliver Cromwell

The luckier people are always open to possibility and don't merely trundle along focussed on the road and goals ahead. They also open themselves to all that is around them on their journey, which is vital in inducing our own good luck.

Knowing when to forego an advantage is as important a lesson in life as learning when to seize an opportunity.

Lucky people have something in common. They don't wait for luck to happen or talk of luck as some magical force. Instead they think and behave in ways that attract good fortune into their lives.

Can we really hope to be met with luck if we go through life carrying an attitude of never expecting good fortune?

It is within anyone's power to squeeze something positive out of misfortune or to turn life's lemons into lemonade, but it is those that try to get lemonade out of a rock who strike oil!

Ask yourself: Do I consider myself unlucky or lucky?

Ask yourself how you came to be who you are today and to be with those who are around you and doing the work that you do. Is it just a series of chances and strokes of luck? Or could it be because of choices you made, decisions you faced, and actions you took?

Some folks have all the luck but it wasn't something they were born with. They developed the ability within themselves to create it and so can we all. They say that it is far better to be lucky than smart. If you believe you were born lucky, chances are you'll depend on that notion, journey on looking for your luck, and fall in and out of good and bad times throughout your entire life. The smarter people among us rely on themselves and keep their eyes open for every little opportunity that comes along.

Lucky events based entirely upon chance do not consistently happen to the same people. Everyone who takes part stands a chance of being the "lucky" winner.

Use every opportunity to invite and include new, inspiring, and influential people into your network. Good luck brings laughter and joy. Bad luck is only funny when it is not happening to us.

When God created mankind, do you honestly believe he had two conveyor belts—one filled with people he'd created for whom everything would be rosy, and the other for those whom he intended everything to go awry?

Dedicate some time to yourself. Give yourself the opportunity each day or each week to sit down and consciously note down everything that went well, the things that paid off, that you could consider lucky, ignoring all the other stuff. Then count them up every now and then and you will soon see that things are not as black as you tend to paint them.

Open yourself to and maximize what's around you.

When opportunity knocks, it can only become lucky if you choose to answer the door.

There's a big distinction between chance and luck. Chance can lead to us winning a prize draw where all we had to do was buy a ticket, but it's not something that we can repeat over and over again. The bigger the prize, the luckier we are perceived to be, and the luckier we feel, but it is a one off.

Within reason and without becoming reckless, open yourself to new experiences. Try a few things that are new to you that you would usually avoid taking part in.

There are, without doubt, people who consider themselves to be consistently blessed with good fortune who, perhaps through modesty, put it down to luck, when all along it is something to do with how they approach life—they seem to make their own luck.

In truth, there is very little in our lives that is entirely down to chance. We have more control over what happens to us moment to moment and day to day than we are inclined to imagine.

Use this opportunity of a moment to contemplate this: to be a lucky person, all one has to do is alter one's way of thinking in order to lead life differently from what one has hitherto considered an unlucky existence. If stuck in the same old routine, break out of it and open your life out a bit more.

When you bash a nail into a wall and hit a water pipe, is it really bad luck? Another person may prepare slightly differently and successfully drive in the nail and miss the pipe. The first person may regard this as "better luck" but the second person made events go that way.

Take control of the situation and never dwell on your own misfortune.

Develop your peripheral vision and a mode of peripheral thinking. Some people are so focussed on a singular goal (sometimes the wrong one) that they cannot see all the exciting ideas and opportunities around them.

Every single successful person, organization, business, or industry has become that way by avoiding following a strict path, and by taking opportunities and the best route at any time.

Two ambitious men go to the same party. Both are impressed by the same woman. One immediately makes his move to win her attention and spends the entire evening trying to impress her, but she shrugs off his efforts and he goes home dejected. The other man mingles and makes several new friends, a couple of good business contacts, exchanges a friendly smile with the woman, and receives invitations to two more parties over the coming weeks, both of which she will attend.

Unlucky thinking might lead a person who is involved in a car crash to believe they are terribly unlucky, that bad things always happen to them. Lucky thinking would commence from the moment of impact with the belief that it is a blessing to come away from it alive.

Those who consider themselves unlucky often share many experiences and factors with those who consider themselves extremely lucky. The only difference between the two groups is their attitude.

Any wreck, disaster, failure, or misfortune we can walk away from gives us the opportunity to live and fight another day.

Luck isn't only a matter of thinking more positively in order to be successful. Luck leads to a greater number of opportunities and therefore a greater chance of success.

We are prisoners of our own making. Opportunity knocks at our door and we're too suspicious to answer it or if we do, by the time we've switched off the burglar alarm and unlocked all the bolts, it has already gone.

Losing does not equate to failure.
A failure is a person who has blundered
and fails to cash in on the experience.

Little opportunities should be improved.
François Fénelon

Even the most burdensome task or loathsome duty can be converted into an interesting opportunity with a simple change of one's viewpoint.

What makes a person great?
The folly of their enemies, the wisdom of their friends, chance, and opportunity.

.

Most are so intent upon looking elsewhere for success that they miss the fact that more often than not it is so close they could reach out and touch it.

Even the smallest opportunity can mark the beginning of a great enterprise.

Everything in life, business, and private life, from the weather to the seasons, is very much made up of patterns. If we open ourselves to these patterns, we will more easily be able to detect them.

Remember that the same defences we put up to keep others out also shut us in.

It waits there for us at the end of the trail, when we run out of energy and purpose, when we believe we cannot go on. That's where opportunity waits with its choices and chances for us to turn over a new leaf and start again.

The pessimist can see only difficulty in every opportunity. The optimist sees opportunity in every difficulty.

Right now a moment is fleeting by!
Capture its reality in paint!
To do that we must put all else out of our
minds. We must become that moment,
make ourselves a sensitive recording
plate. Give the image of what we actually
see, forgetting everything that has been
seen before our time.

Paul Cézanne

**Everyone has a fair turn to
be as great as he pleases.**

Jeremy Collier

Opportunities are like buses— you wait and wait and then three come along all at once.

There is nothing to be gained in living life believing things will get worse. Convince yourself that a brighter future lies ahead and your prophecy could come true.

With vision and a little bit of effort, yesterday's failures can become tomorrow's opportunities.

Real opportunities are right there under your nose if you can avoid the exotic lure of everything distant and difficult.

One must besiege chance, conquer it, and bring it around to serve one's purpose.

It is somehow reassuring to know that luck has been on mankind's mind since before the birth of Christ. Even Nero's tutor, the Roman Stoic philosopher and statesman Seneca believed: "Luck is what happens when preparation meets opportunity." This is still the basis of almost every motivator, life coach, and philosopher on the subject today.

In the middle of difficulty lies opportunity.

Albert Einstein

Luck? I don't know anything about luck. I've never banked on it, and I'm afraid of people who do. Luck to me is something else: hard work—and realizing what is opportunity and what isn't.

Lucille Ball

The right person for any opportunity is the one who recognizes it and seizes it.

Those who see the luck of others as being written in the stars would, on closer inspection, see that those stars were in fact sparks issuing from the grindstone of their endeavors.
So we should always be vigilant and prepared for those moments when opportunity raises its head.

Had I not sinned, what would there be for you to pardon?
My fate has given you the opportunity for mercy.

Ovid

Opportunities do not arrive labeled with their value. They arrive to be challenged and their true worth discovered through time and effort.

A day will come just like other days; and in it will come an hour, exactly like all other hours; and in that hour will be a moment within which the opportunity of a lifetime will face us.

To each their chance.
To each, regardless of their birth,
a shining, golden opportunity; the
right to live, to work, to be oneself
and become whatever vision and
effort combine to create. This is
life's promise to us all.

Everything in life is luck.
                    Donald Trump

Whether they arise open-faced or in disguises, greet opportunities thoughtfully and seek their meanings bravely and earnestly.

A wise person will always seek to create more opportunities than they find.

The only fact that we can be absolutely certain of about luck is that it changes.

When things go wrong, immediately, without hesitation, allow yourself to consider how much worse it could have been.

When we see others miss an opportunity it is not like witnessing someone losing to a better opponent but, more tragically, like watching them lose against themselves.

No matter how big you make the opportunity, someone will always expand to fill it.

The essence of an equal opportunity is not to offer the chance to become the same, but the freedom for everyone to become different and realize his unique potential.

Grab your chances while you can.

Luck is built step by step, in work, in friendship, and in love.

Any power must be an enemy of mankind which enslaves the individual by terror and force... All that is valuable in human society depends upon the opportunity for development accorded to the individual.

Albert Einstein

If you want to succeed in the world, you cannot sit and wait for opportunities to come to you. You must be prepared to make your own opportunities as you go on.

Life is short and opportunities are transient.

A person can have wonderful connections and possess great intelligence, but without the ability to recognize and grasp opportunities when they arise, these remain meaningless gifts.

You don't have to wait for opportunity to come knocking at your door. If you want it badly enough then you can always go and knock on its door.

Treat each failure as an opportunity to begin again, a little wiser than before.

Everyone's task is as unique as their specific opportunity to implement it.

A wise old sage would advise you never to miss a chance to sit down and rest your feet.

Everything comes into our life for a reason. Some of us are luckier than others in that we are able to work out why and know exactly how we should react when they do.

Always be on the lookout and take care to listen, then pay heed to your lucky hunches.

We all have the opportunity to step out of the rut of feeling unlucky. We may have experienced loss, financial or personal, or had things go wrong for us, love turn sour, things break down, but if we look around us we're sure to discover wonderful things that are part of our world: friends, children, colleagues, or accomplishments, for all of which we can be grateful and which should serve to make us feel exceptionally lucky.

Turn your misfortunes into the fuel for your resolve to achieve better results.

In order to get through life feeling lucky it is important not to constantly focus our attention on the unlucky aspects of our lives and begin to take note of the positive facets. Soon one will be able to look back and see that all manner of good and better things have happened.

Written in Chinese, the word "crisis" is composed of two characters. One represents danger and the other represents opportunity.

John F. Kennedy

Lessons in opportunity abound in nature. Watch the flowers when they bloom—the bees will arrive.

Consider the mosquito never invited. She never waits for an opening—she makes one.

It is true that one can present people with opportunities but it is also true that one cannot make people equal to them.

There's no excuse—every day is stuffed to the brim with opportunities: to be honest, to be friendly, to be ourselves.

If you're a fisherman and lucky enough to come across a hungry man you can catch a fish and you can sell it to him. If, on the other hand, he's lucky enough for you to choose to teach him to fish, you ruin a wonderful business opportunity!

There is an old saying that if you can see the bandwagon you've missed it.

There are four things that never come back to us. The words we speak, the shots we fire, our past life, and all the neglected opportunities.

The same sun rises for us all.

To go through life and not see any opportunities is rather like walking through the forest and never seeing any firewood.

Success requires training and discipline and hard work. If you're not frightened by these things, the opportunities are as many as they ever were.

It's not the follies
we have committed
during our lifetime
that we regret.
It's the ones we didn't
commit when we had
the opportunity that
give us most grief.

**Get up and look for
the circumstances
you want, and if you
can't find them, then
make them.**

Much opportunity is
lost by deliberation.

**It's each person's
choice of course
but better to make the
most of what comes
than what goes.**

God can only supply
the opportunity.
He cannot take
advantage of it for us.

People think that at the top there isn't much room. They tend to think of it as an Everest. My message is that there is tons of room at the top.

Margaret Thatcher

Procrastination is the grave in which opportunity is buried.

Opportunity should be met with feeling and the desire to use it to leave you and the world better for it.

Every minute holds a new opportunity to start over.

**Try to always look on the bright side.
The worst it can do is give you eyestrain.**

Seeing an ambulance is considered very unlucky by some, unless you pinch your nose or hold your breath or until you see a black or a brown dog. If you don't see one and follow this strange custom you'll be lucky if another ambulance passes in time to rescue you!

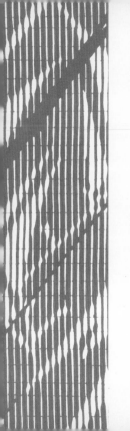

Intuition and gut reactions
are never to be ignored.
They can often lead us to
making the correct and
most effective decisions
and choices.

**When opportunity
lays the world at
your feet, you had
better make sure
you can find your
shoes.**

There is rarely a lack of opportunity. When you feel as though there is, you are more likely to be experiencing a lack of purpose or direction.

Arrange whatever pieces come your way.

Virginia Woolf

Where there is an open mind and a certain willingness, there will always be a new frontier of opportunity.

The quality of any enterprise is equal and proportionate to the quality of the minds behind it.

Too much organization can often ruin opportunity, for organization is the ruin of improvisation.

Every translation is unfaithful to the original and every original is unfaithful to the translation but both have the opportunity to shine.

One must pass
through the
circumference of time
before arriving at the
center of opportunity.

Baltasar Gracián

Think "opportunity"
and you'll be
thinking lucky
thoughts.

Did you hear about the woman who confused her tranquilizers with her birth control pills? She now has a dozen kids but isn't in the slightest bit bothered about it.

Originality comes from using one's opportunities to explore uncharted territory. One has to hike there—you can't thumb a ride.

When we focus our thoughts on a brighter future, it can help us to face any failure that may arise with positive optimism and the drive to persist in our efforts.

The worst form of bad luck to fall victim to is the foolhardy belief that nothing is well done except that which you do yourself.

Man should measure by his own appreciation the originality of his works and deeds. For otherwise he risks suffering the bad luck of falling victim to that folly which makes people applaud imitation and hiss at the real thing.

Published by MQ Publications Limited
12 The Ivories, 6–8 Northampton Street
London N1 2HY
Tel: 020 7359 2244   Fax: 020 7359 1616
email: mail@mqpublications.com

ISBN (10)   1-84601-115-9
ISBN (13)   978-1-84601-115-3

1 3 5 7 9 0 8 6 4 2

Printed and bound in China